Sergej Jensen

Dogs

AF412421

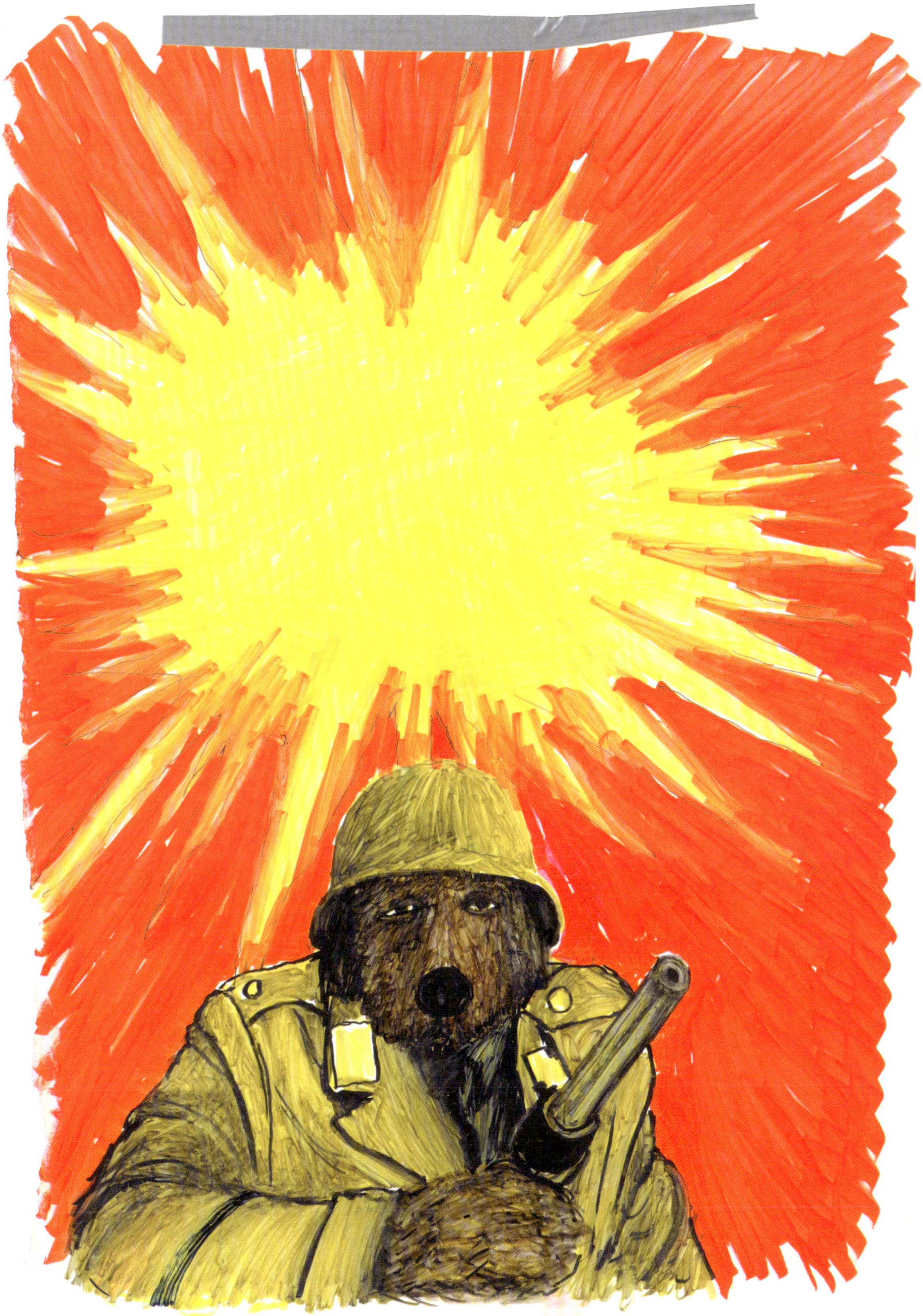

PORK SALAD PRESS

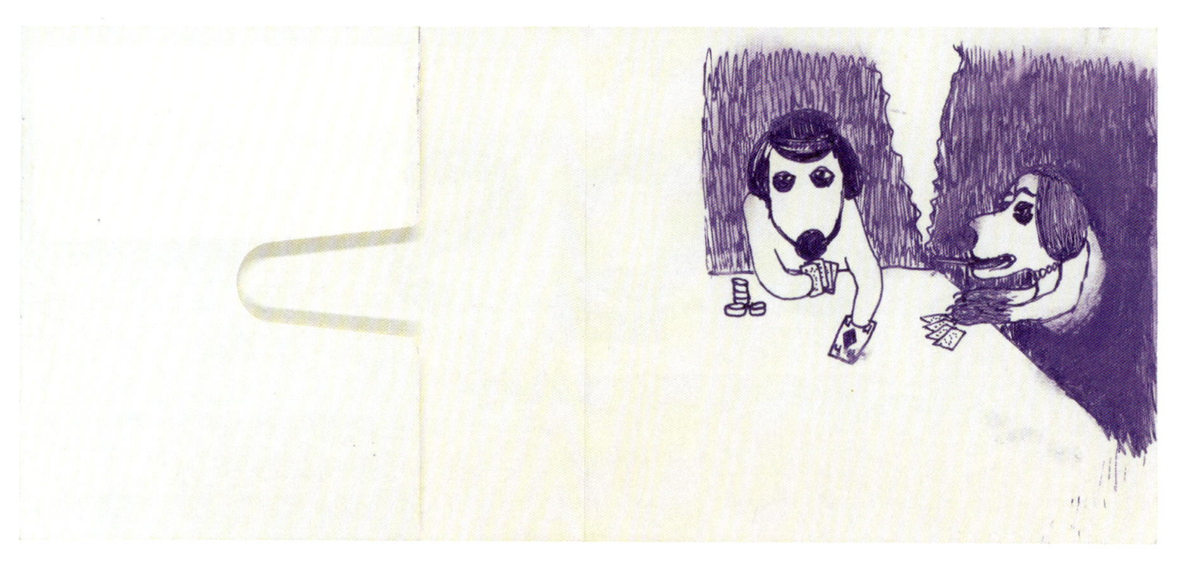
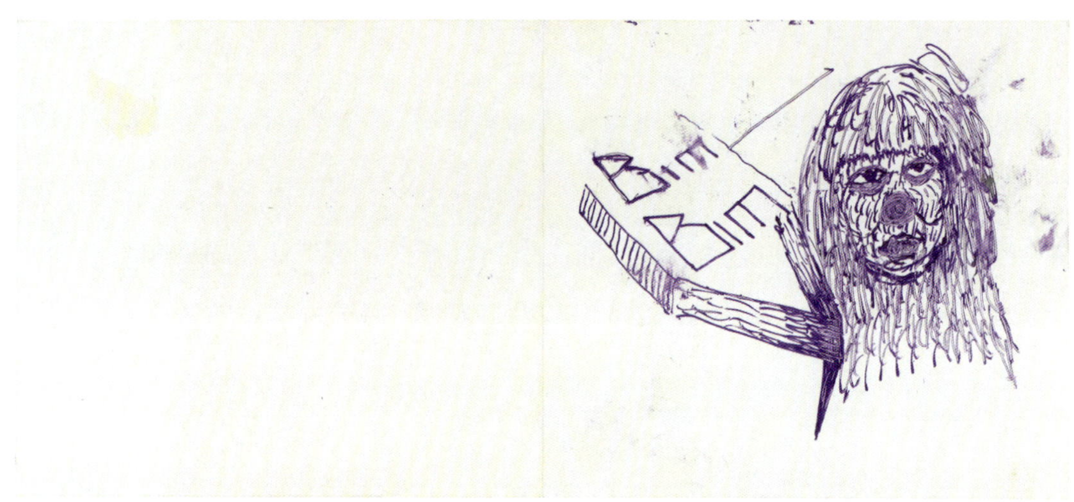
BIT
BIT

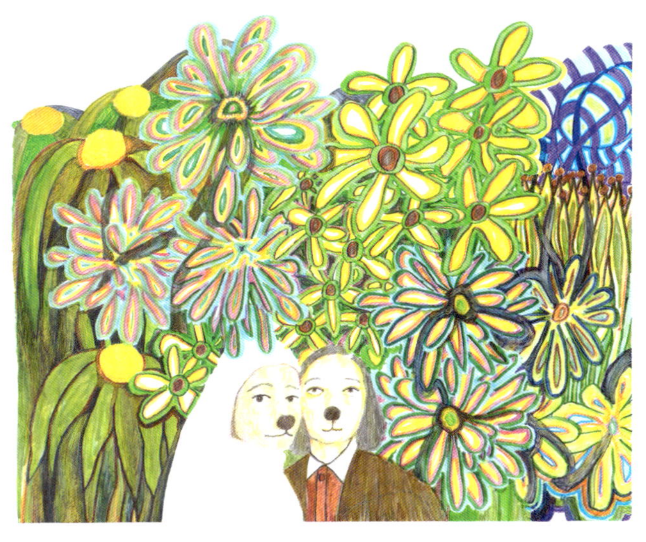

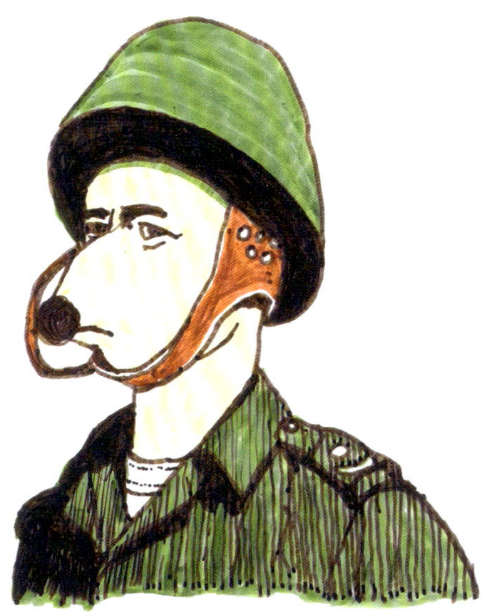

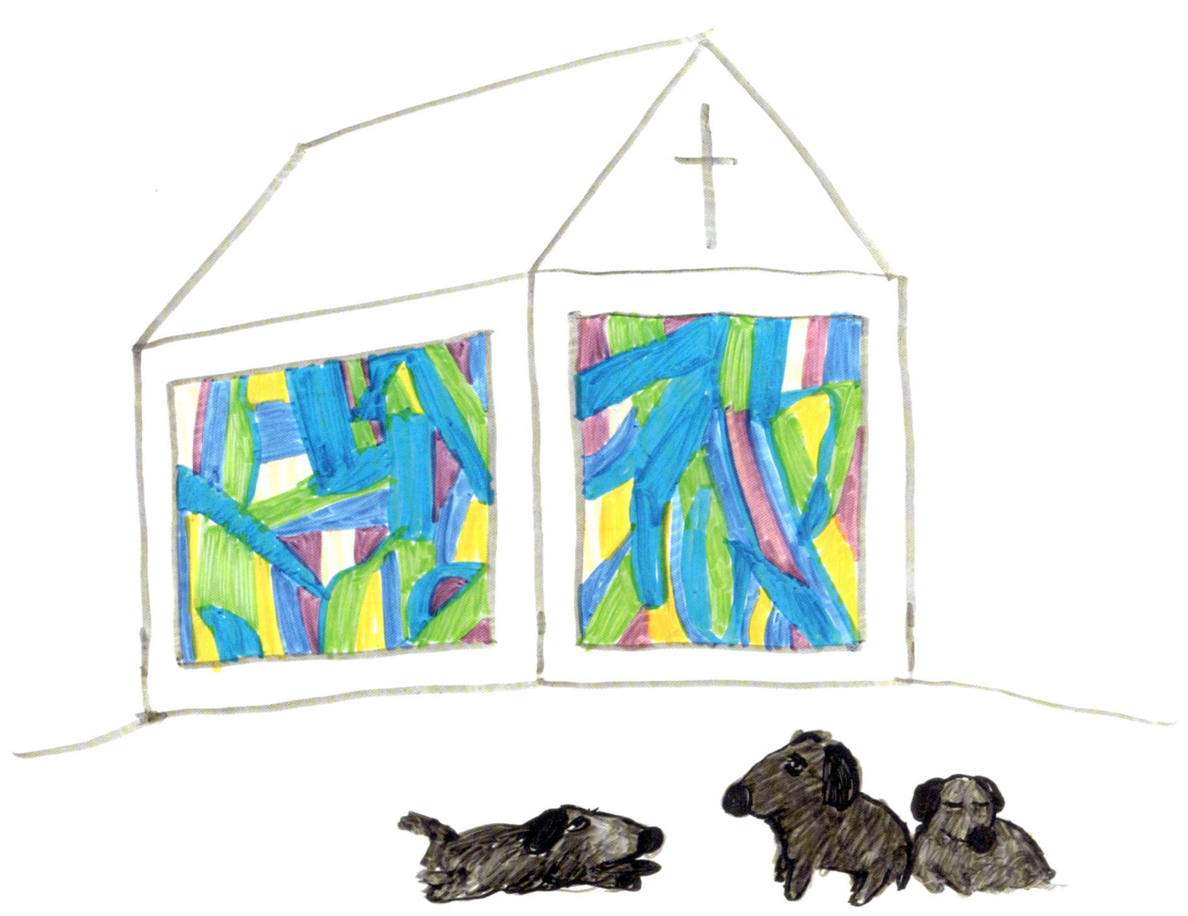

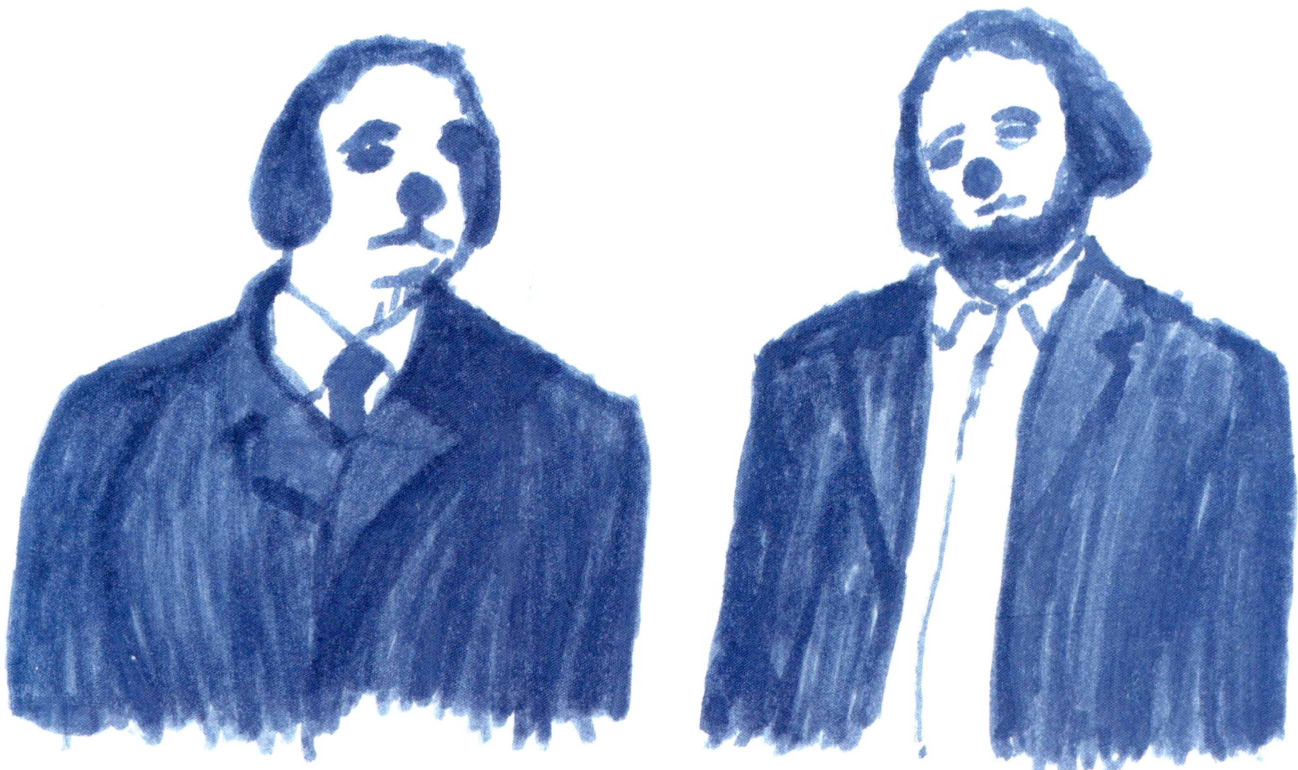

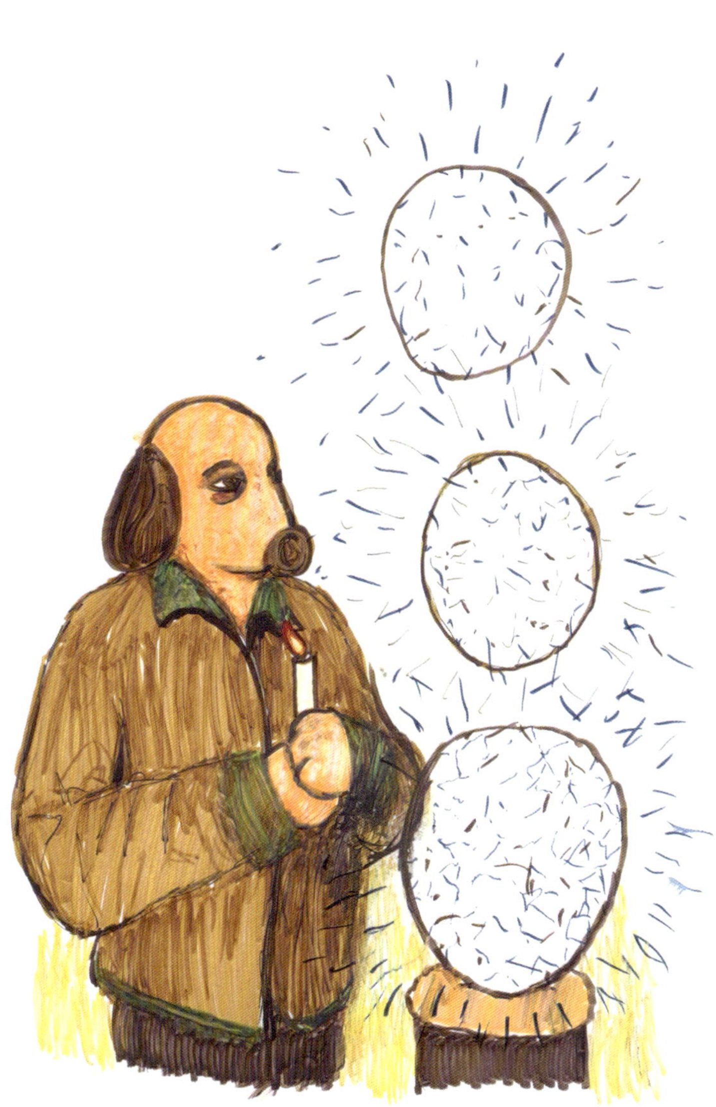

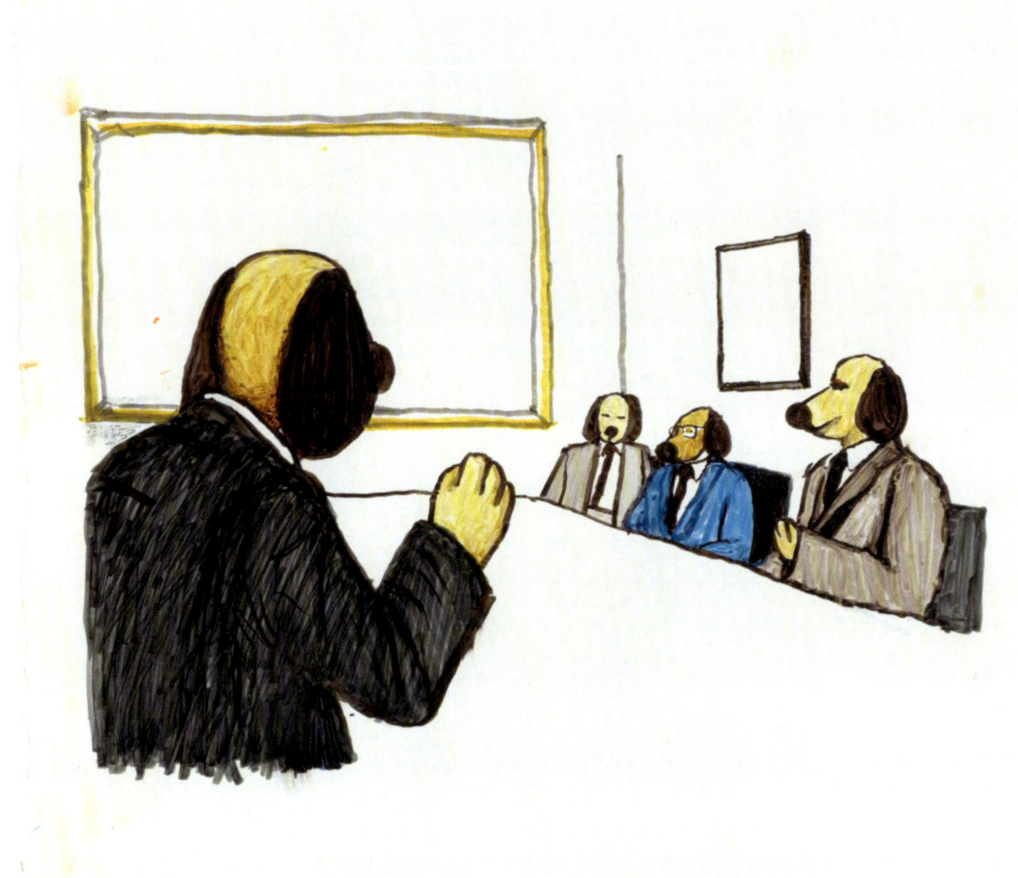

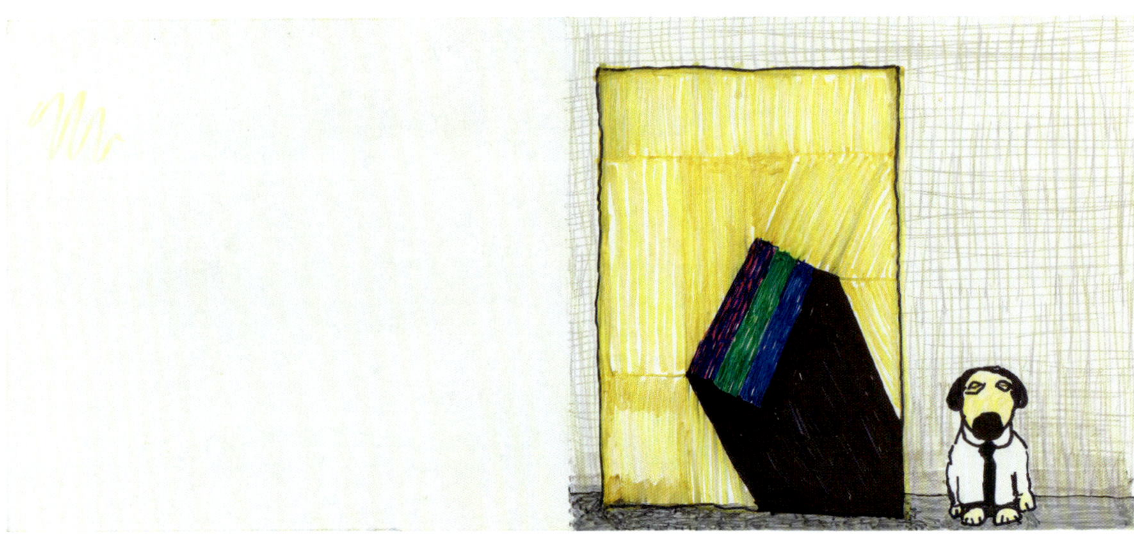

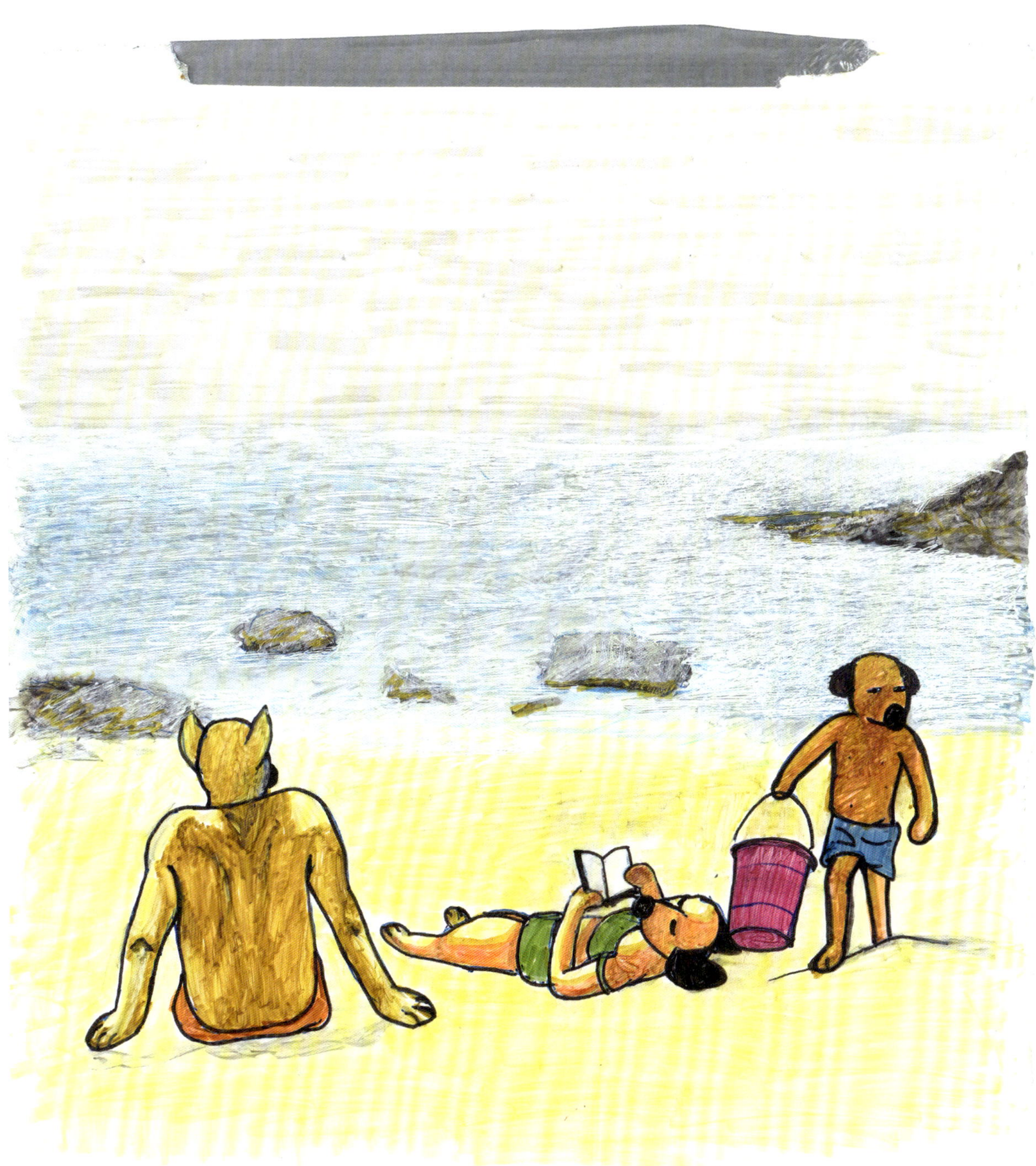

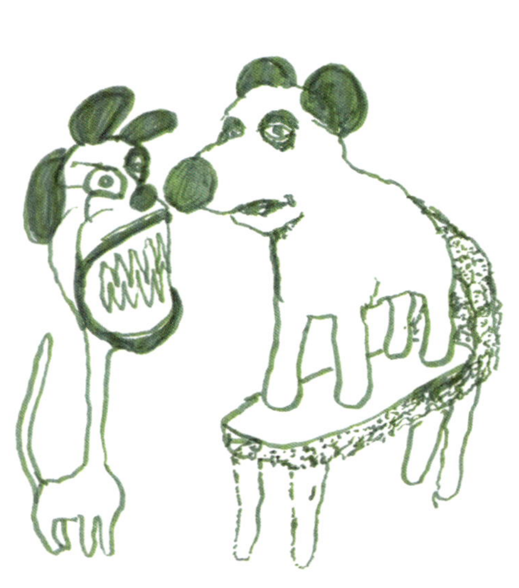
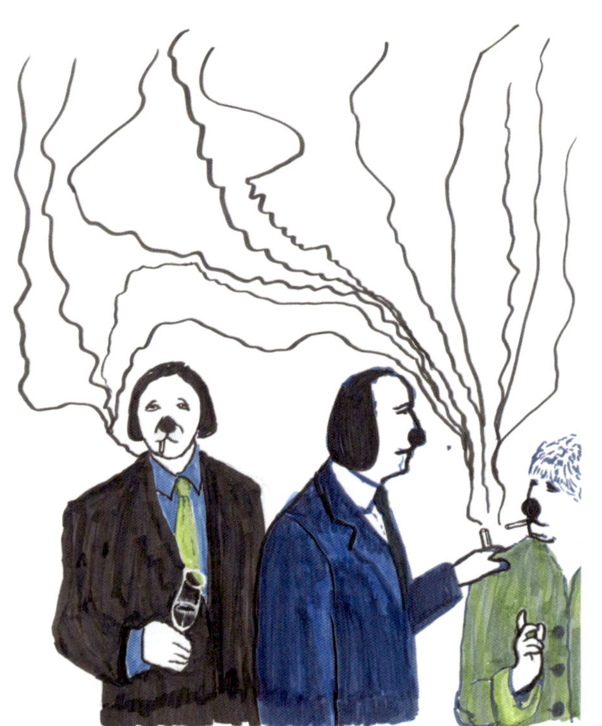
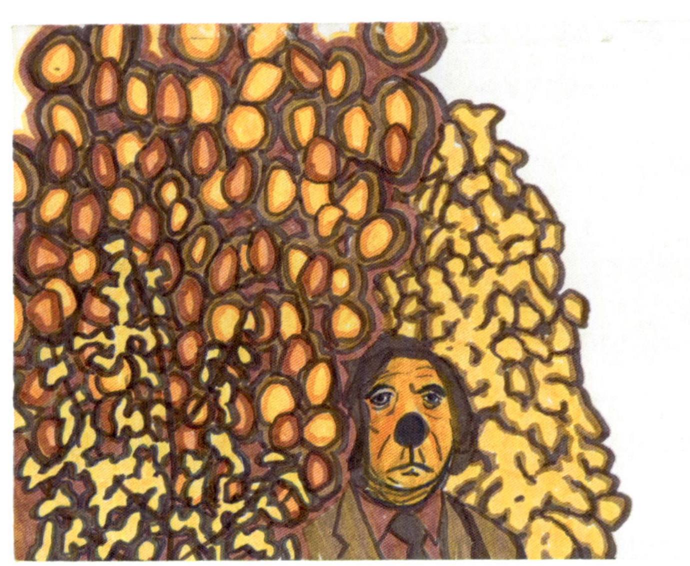
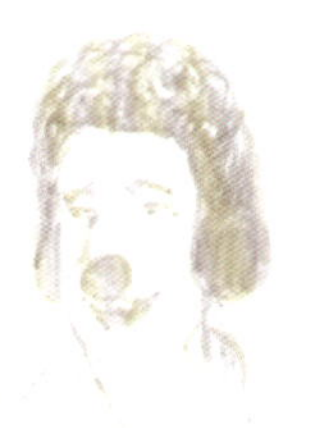
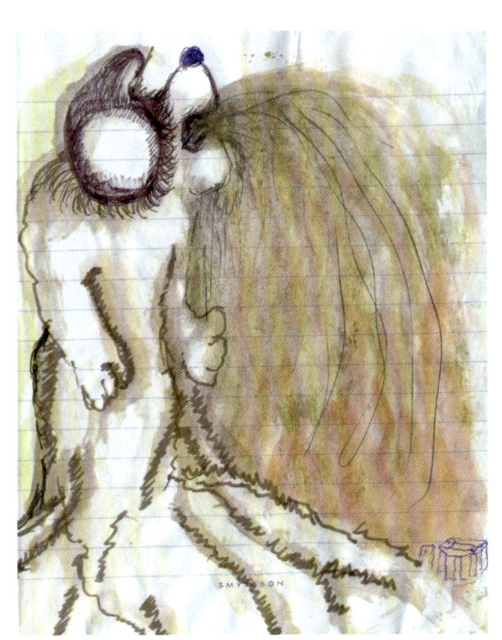

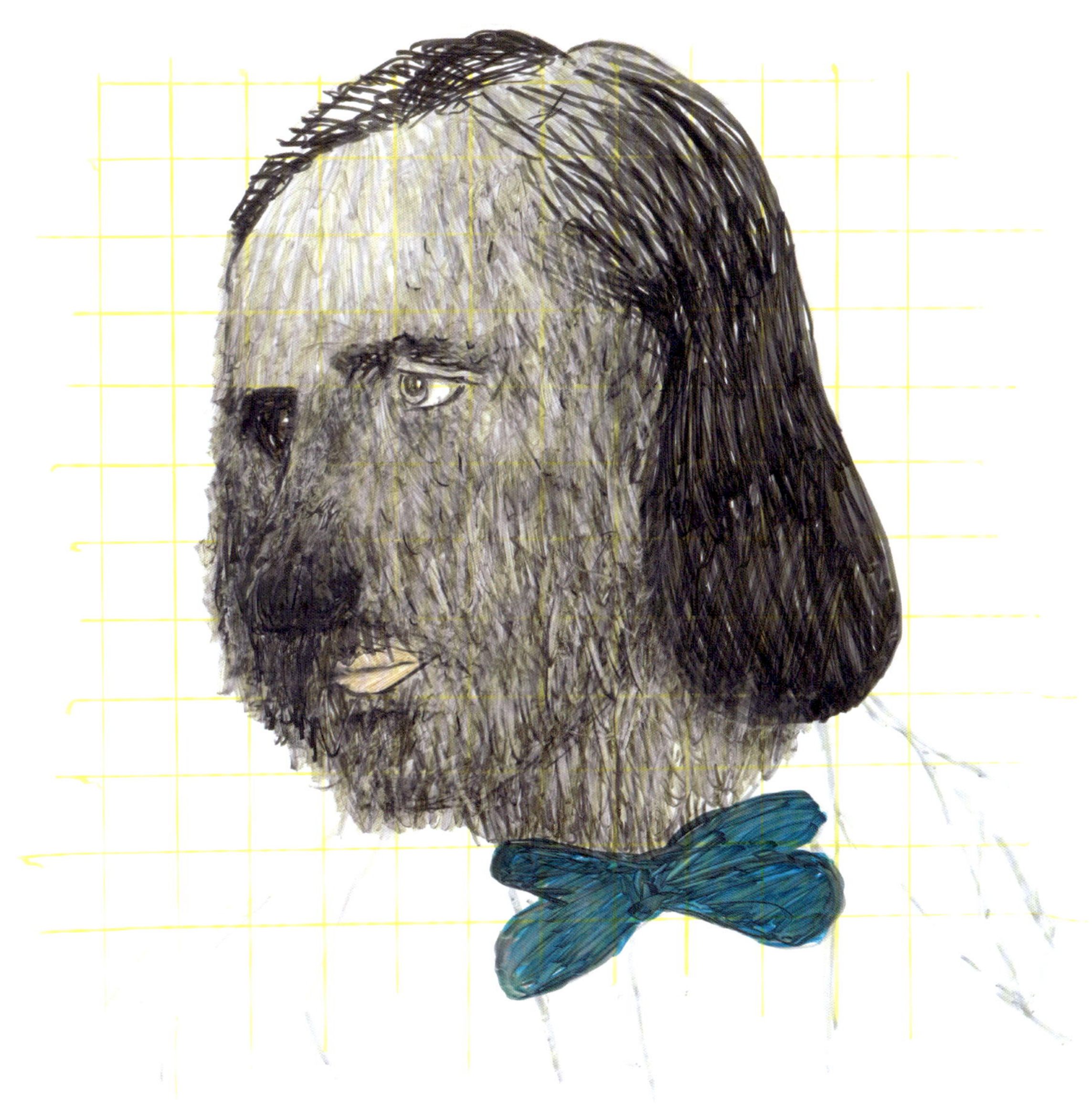

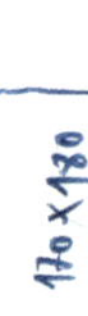

170 x 180

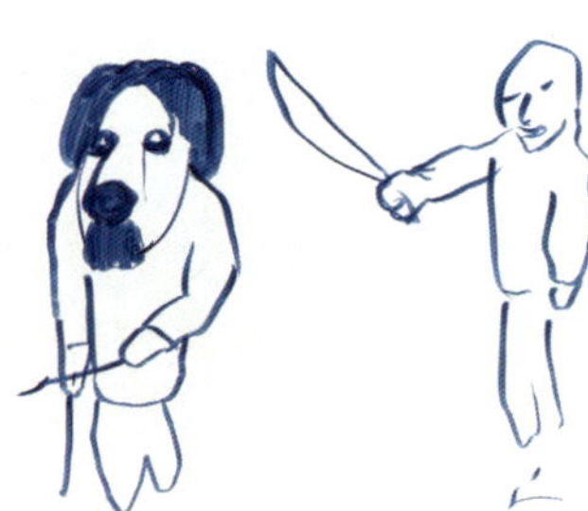

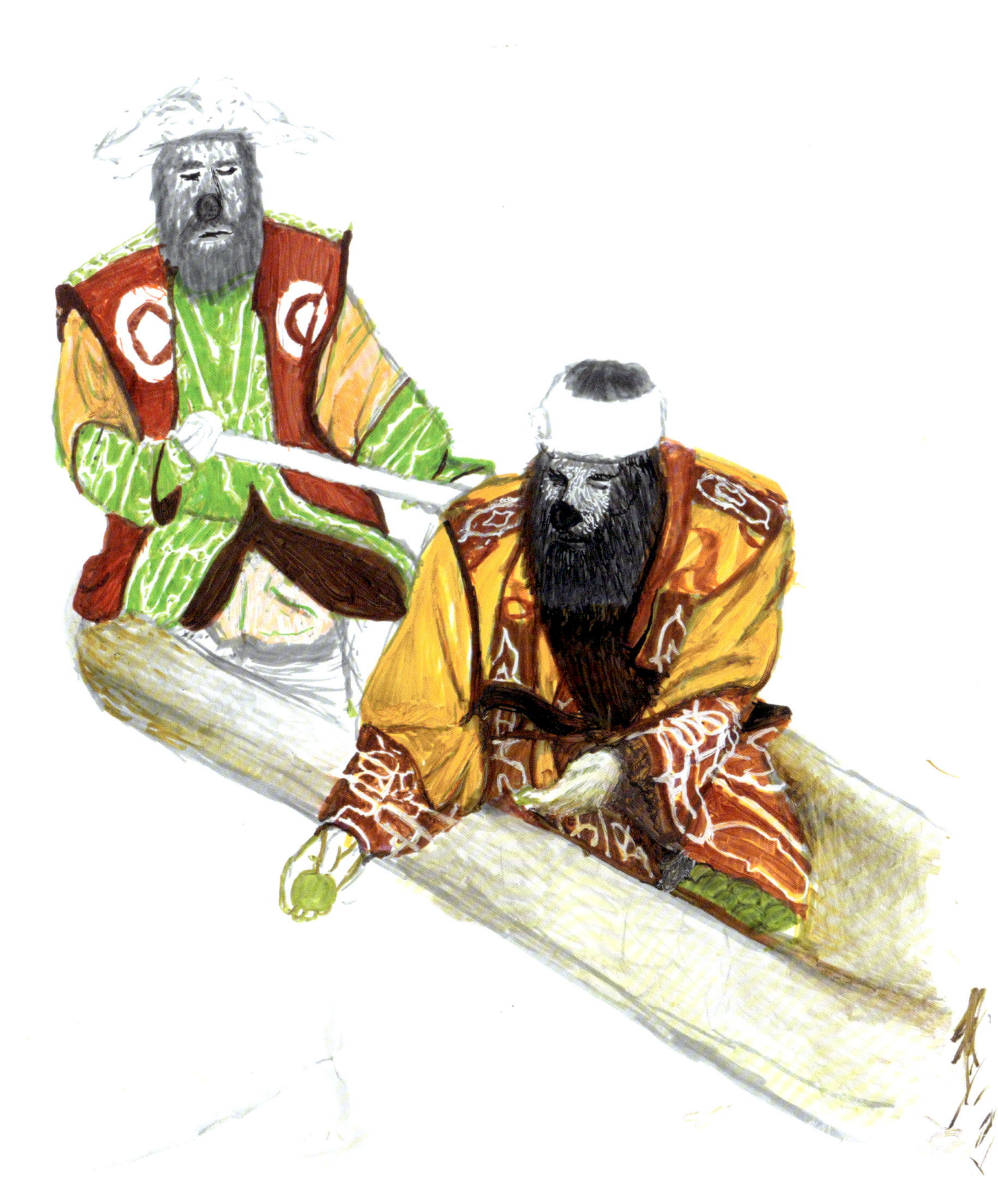

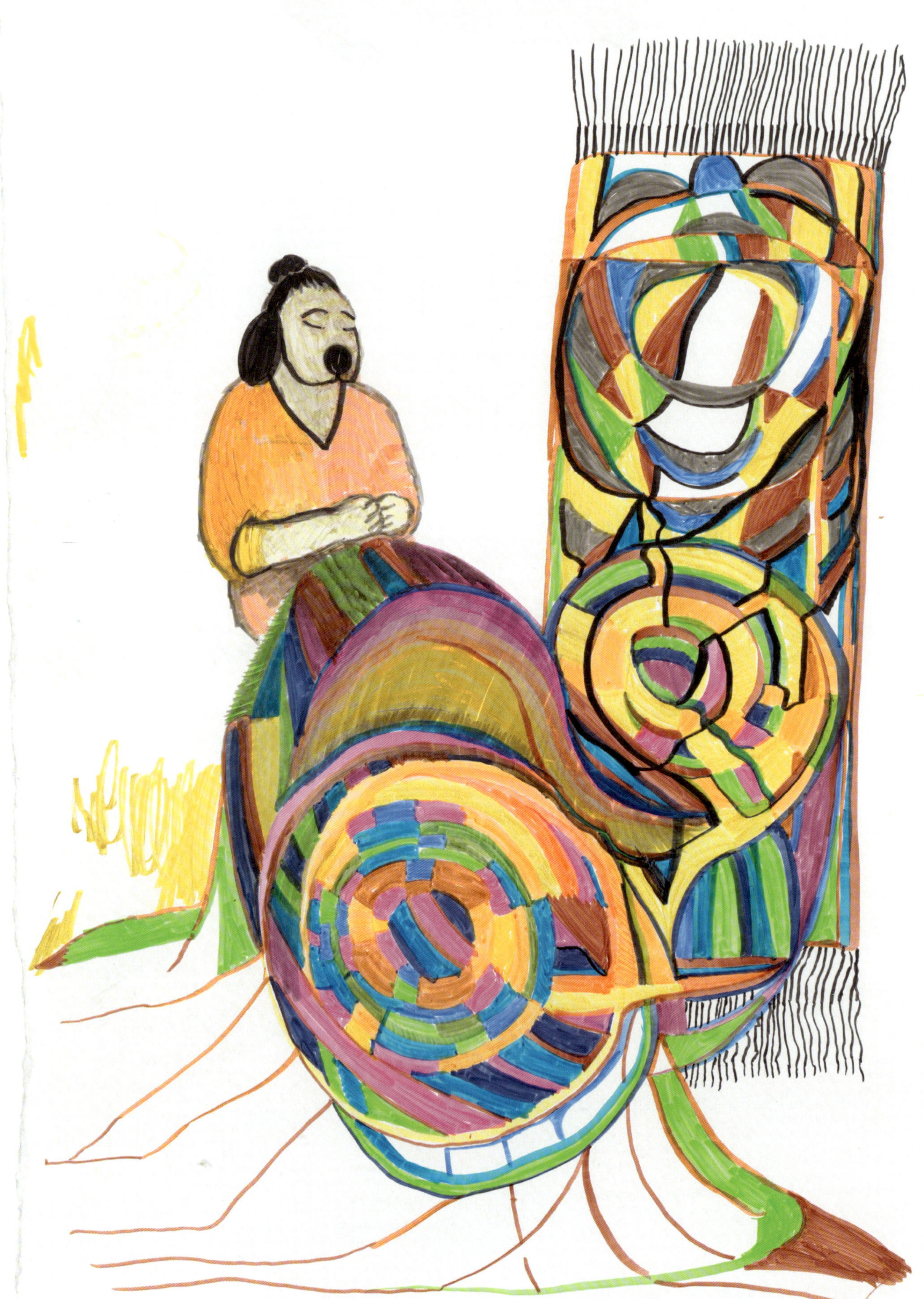

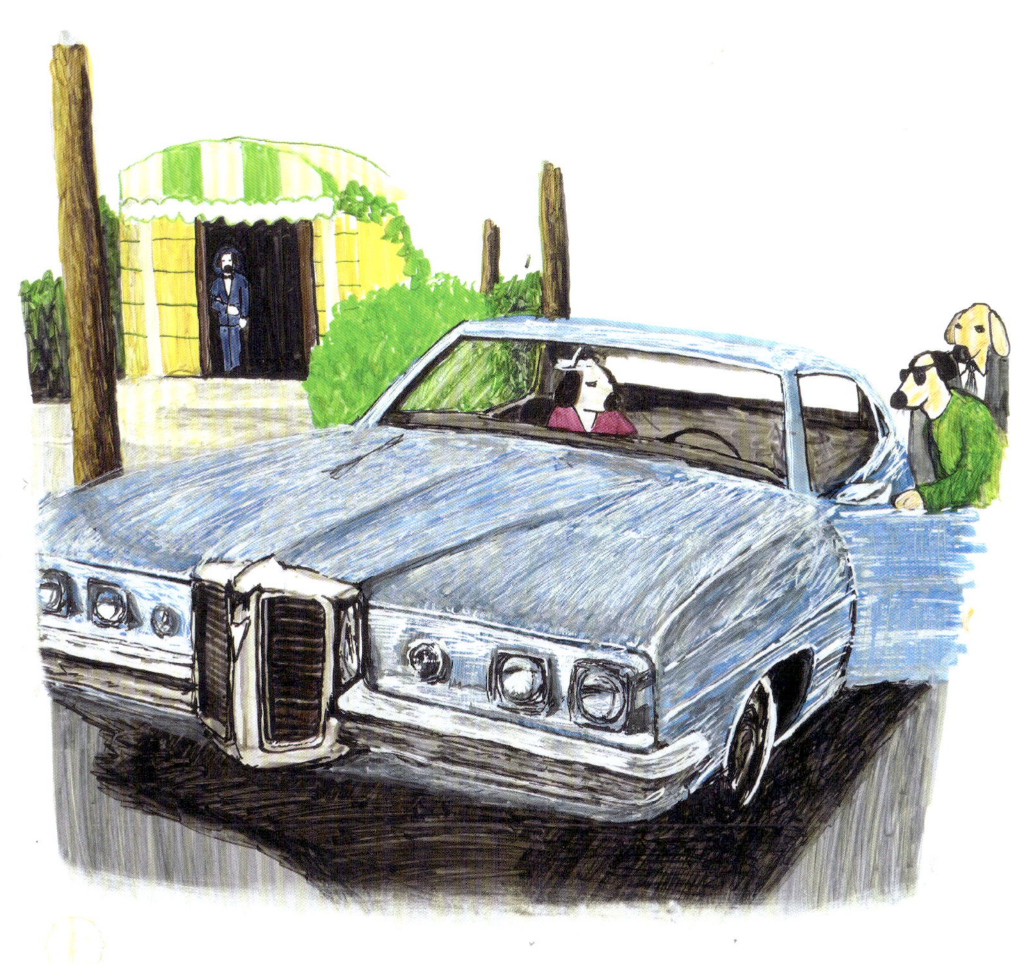
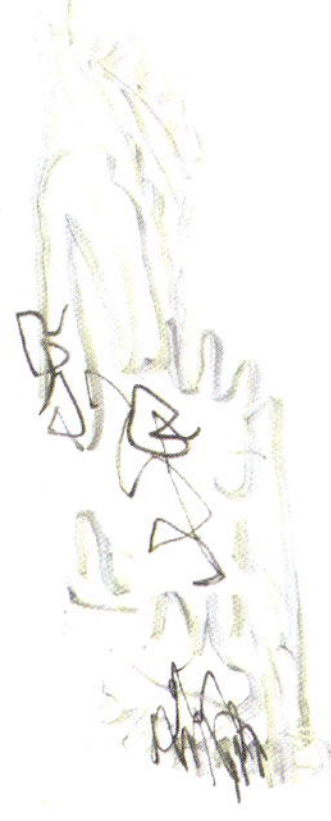

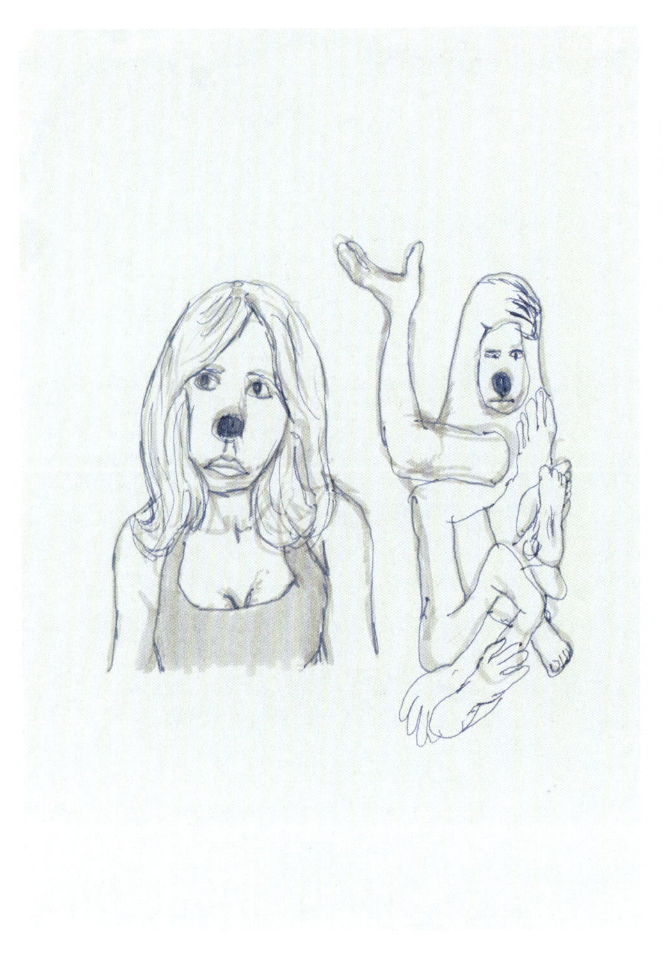

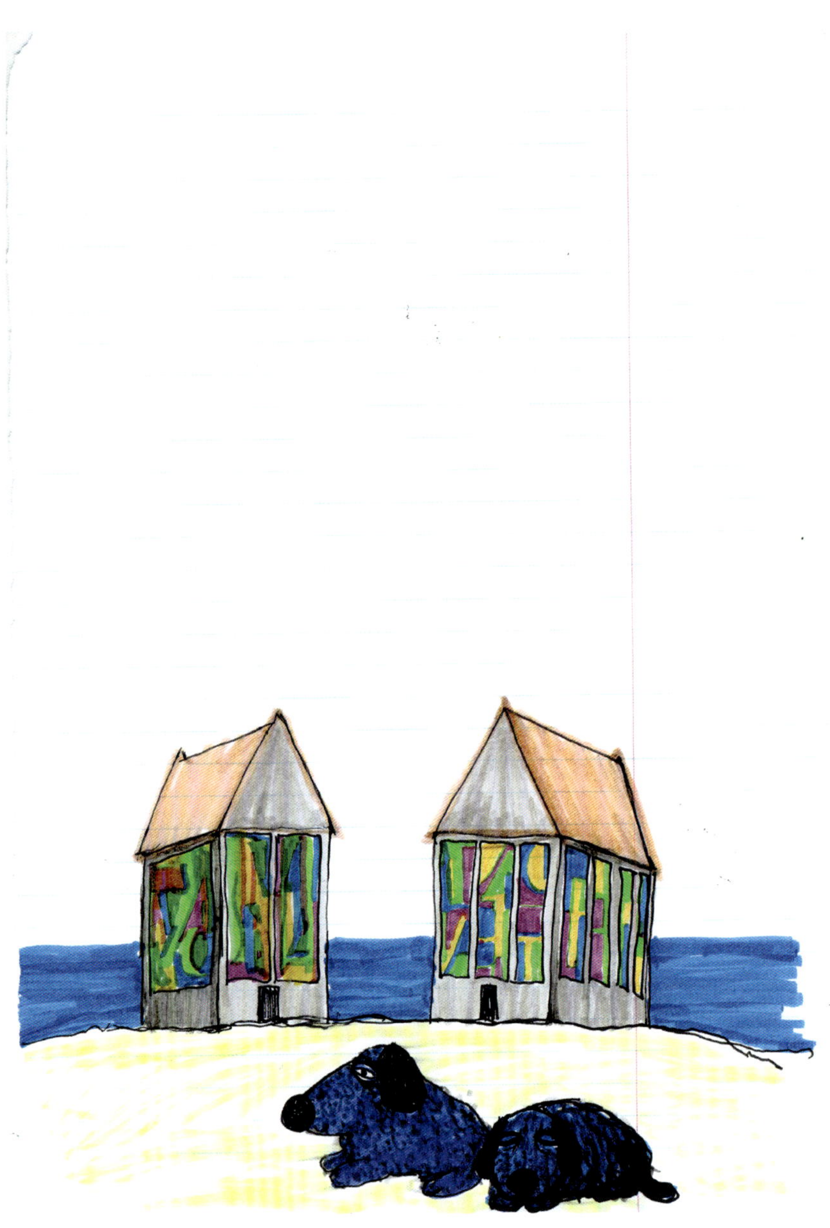

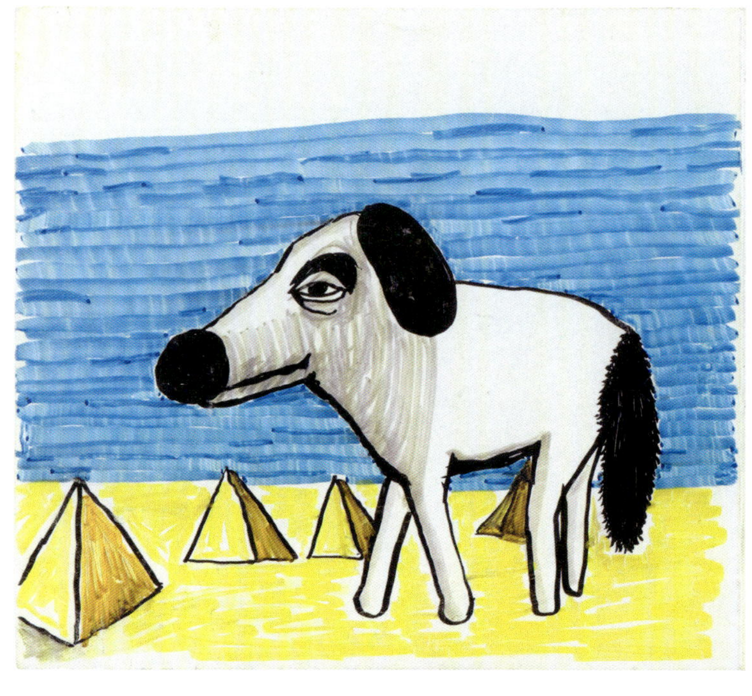

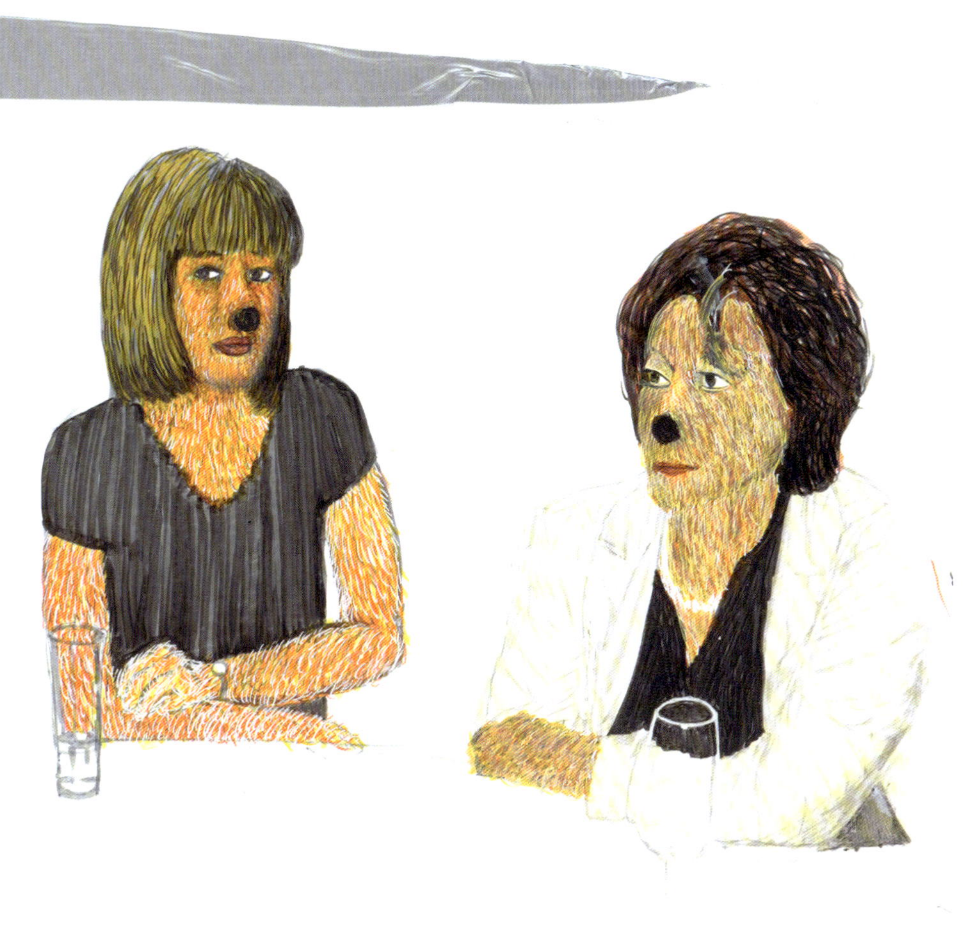

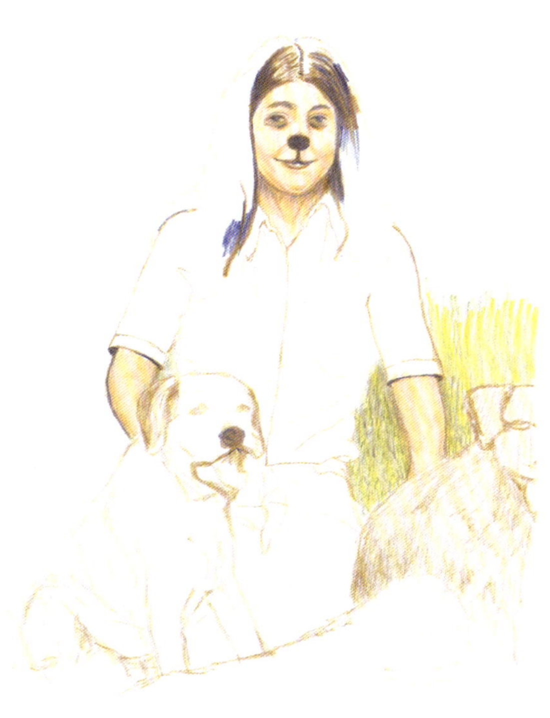

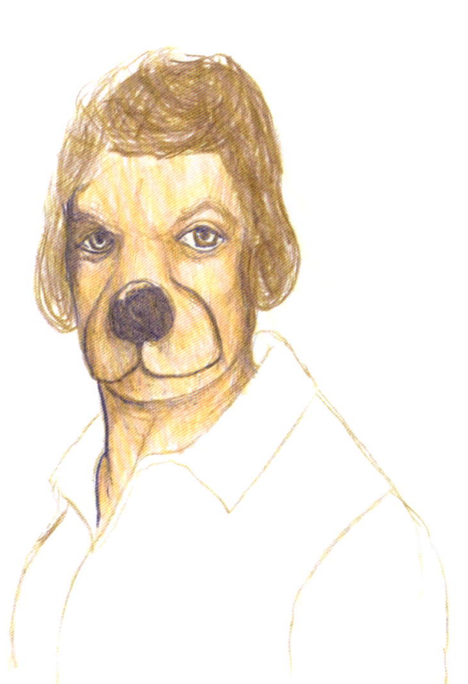

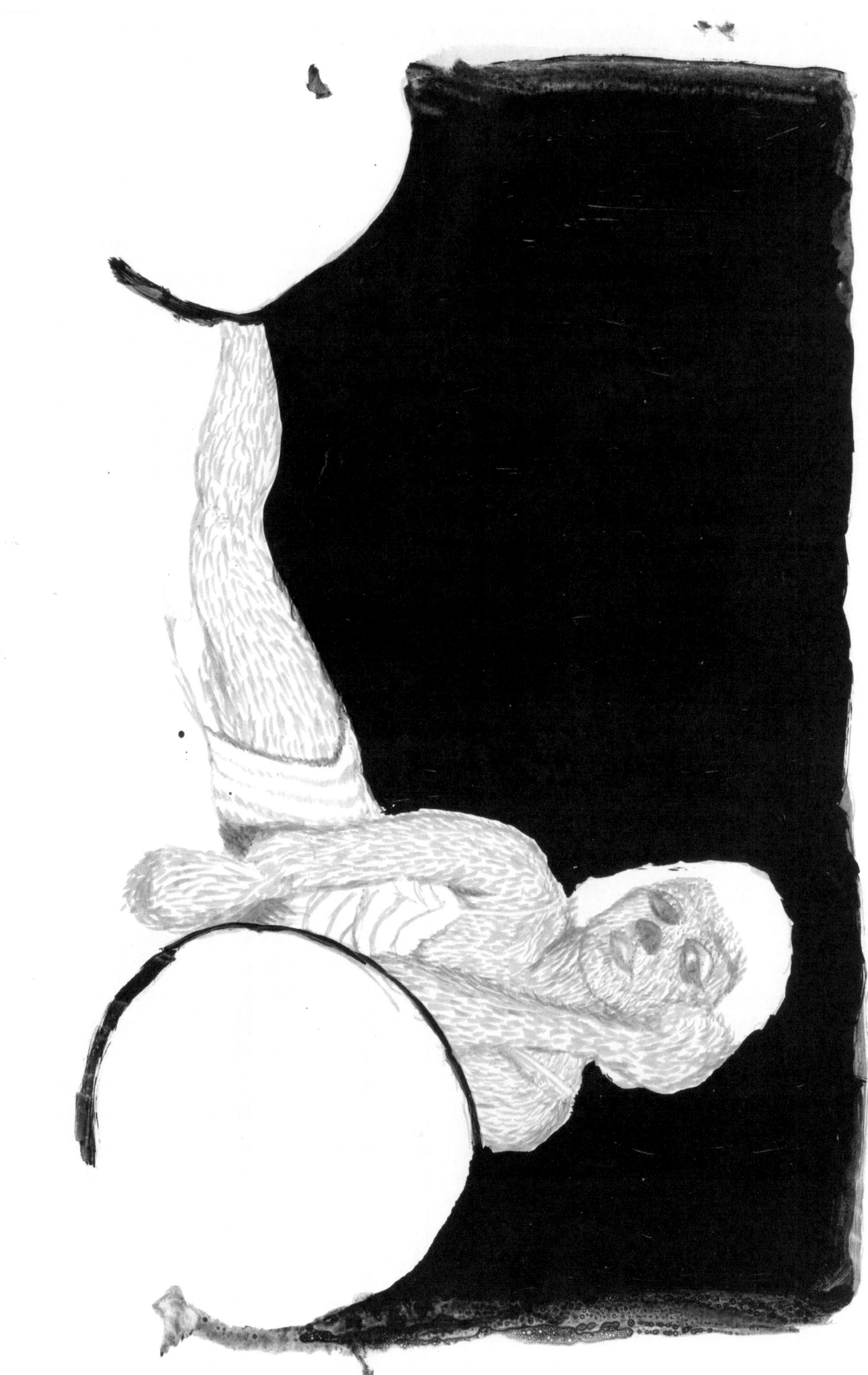

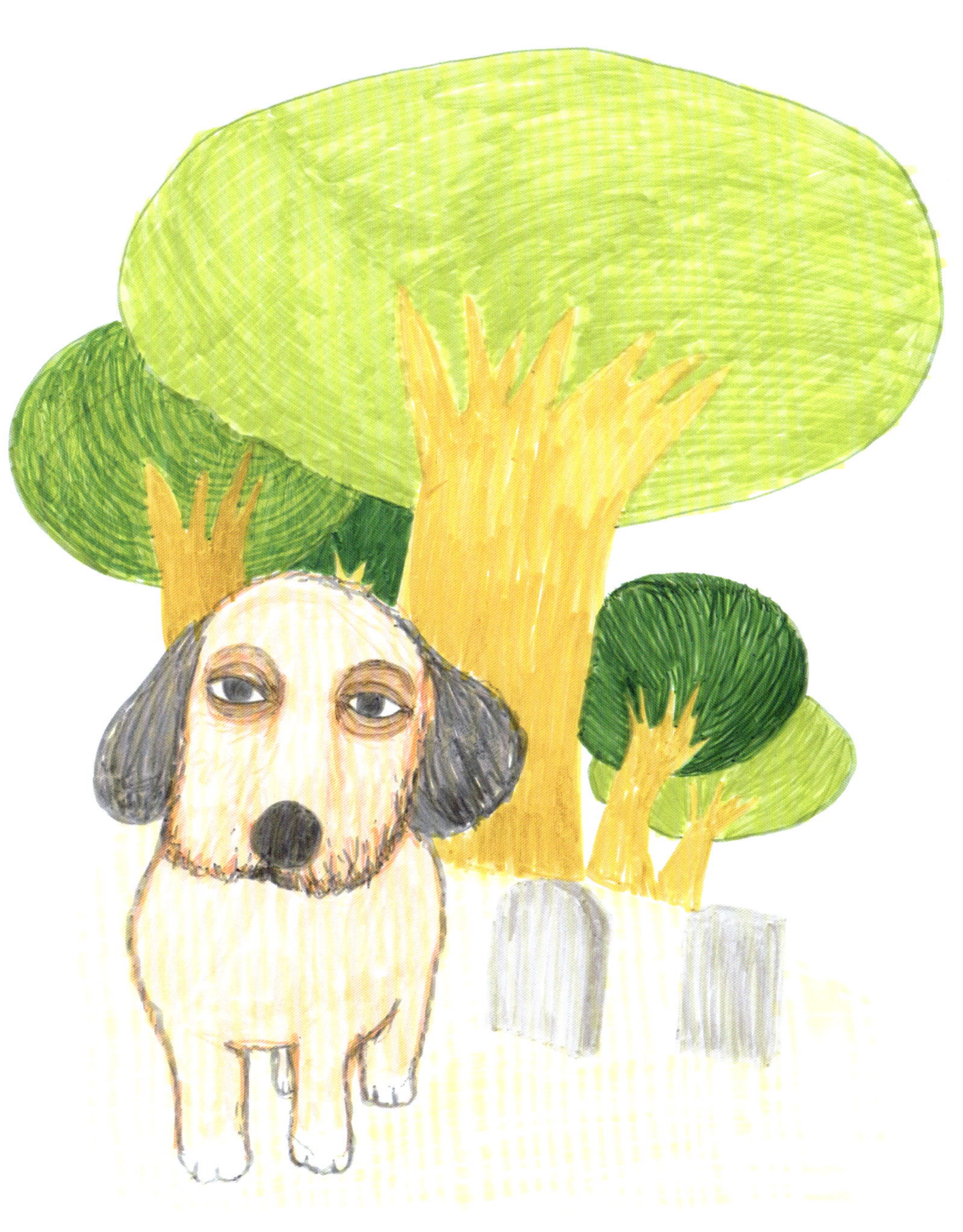

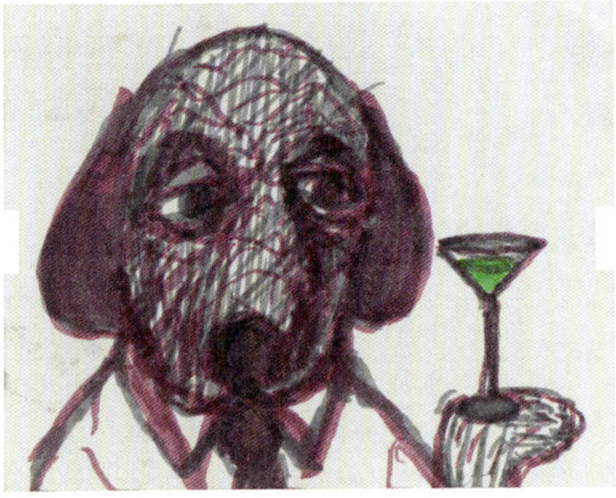

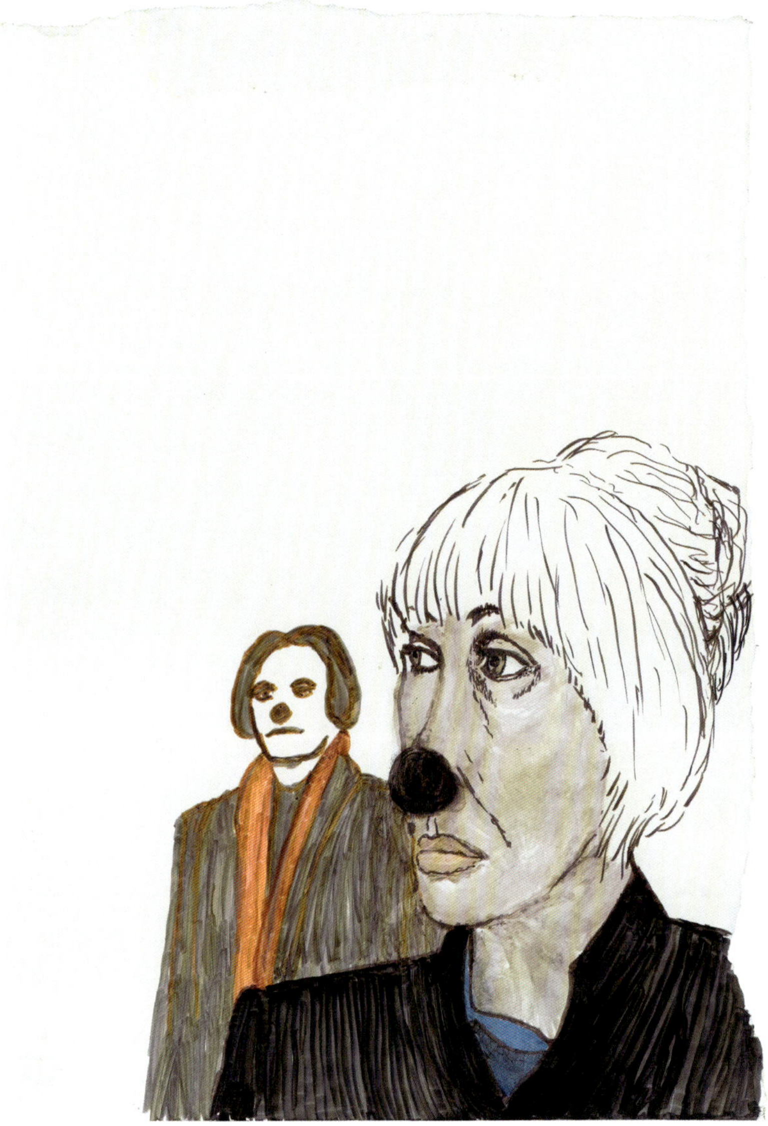

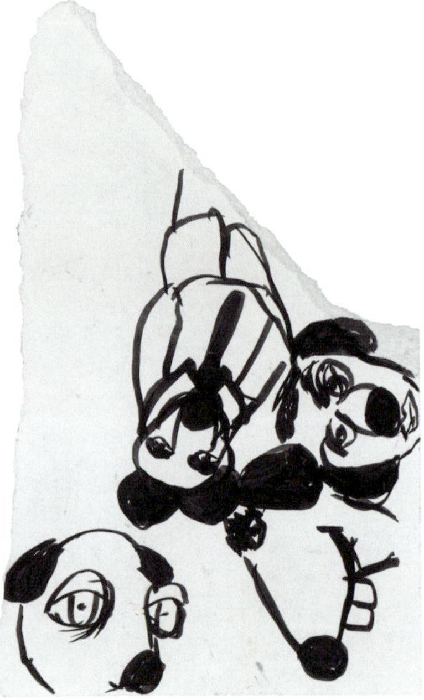

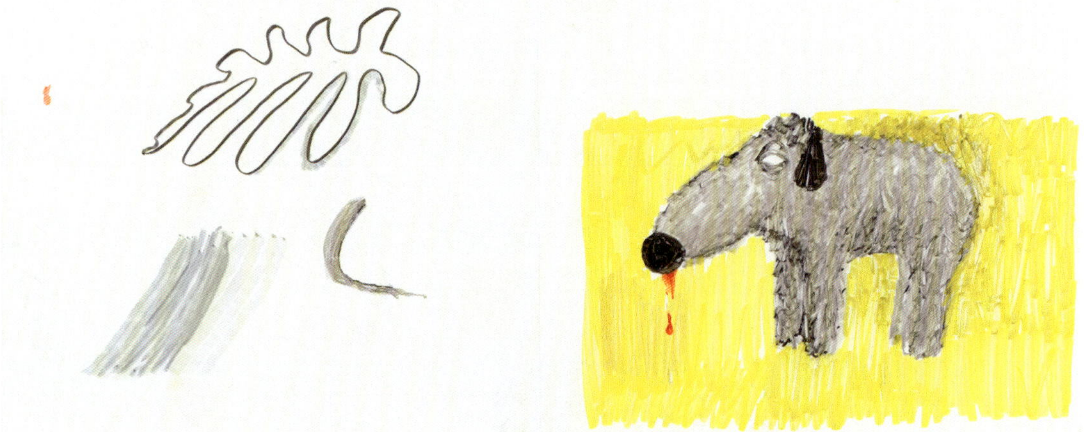

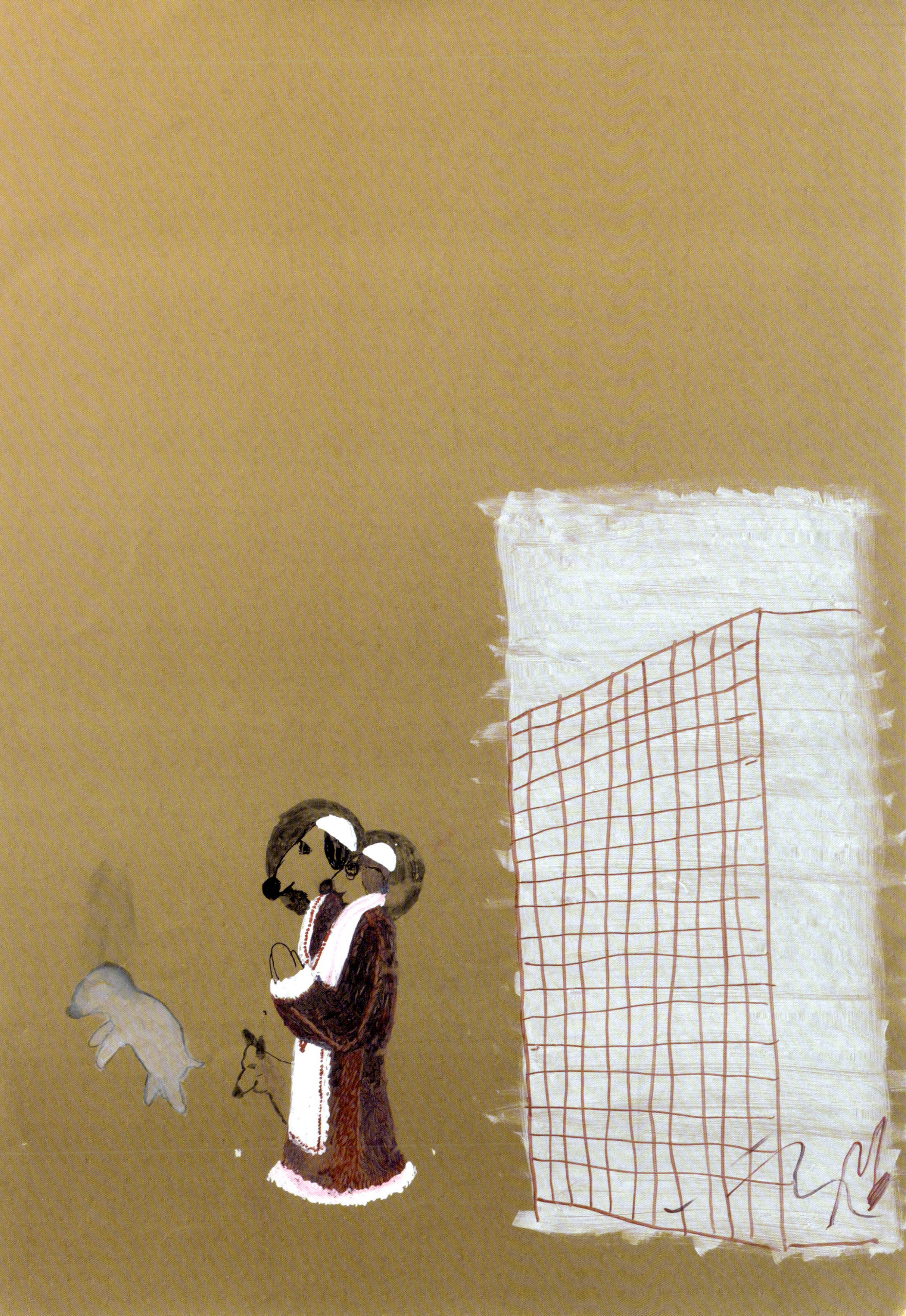

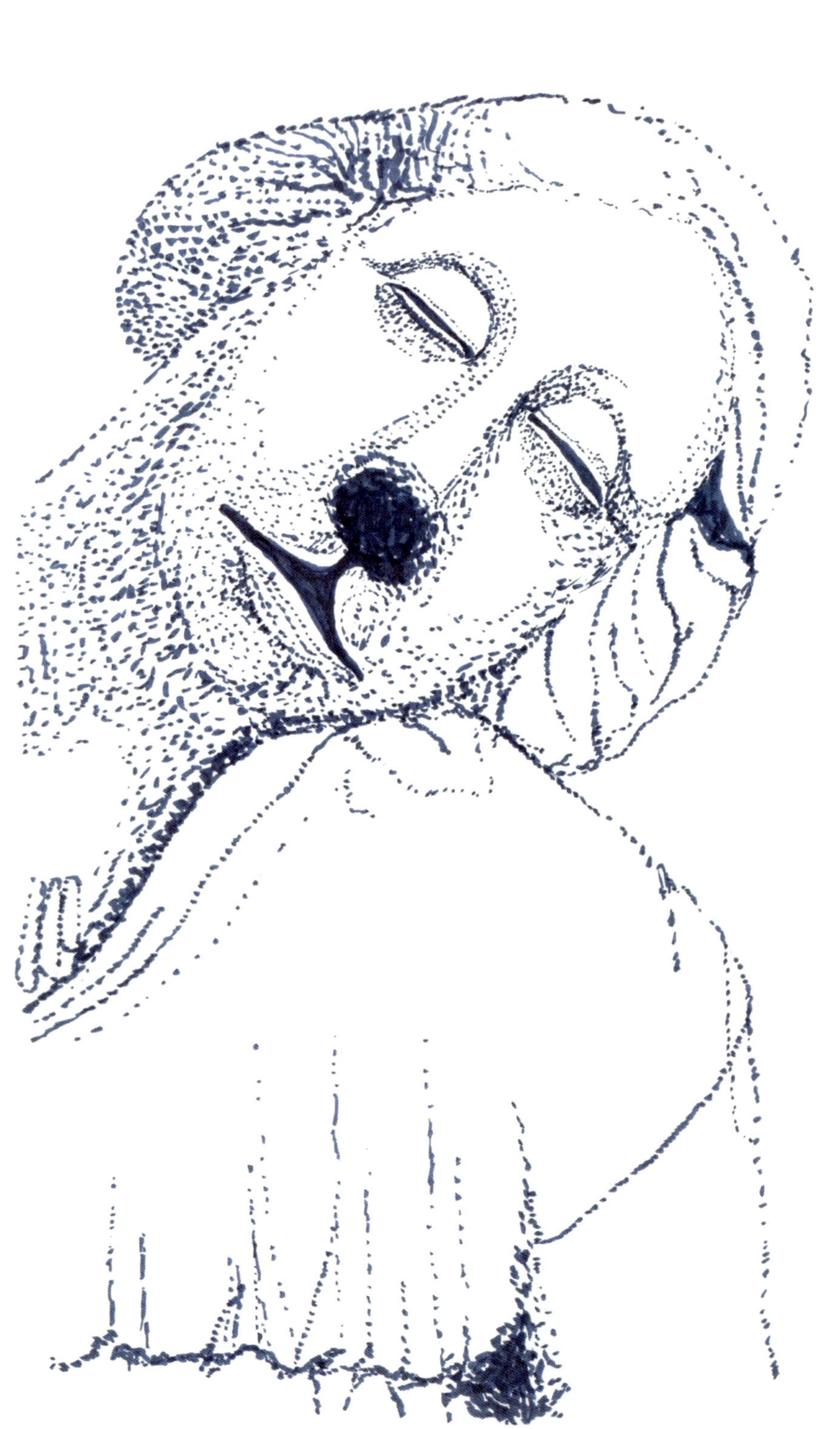

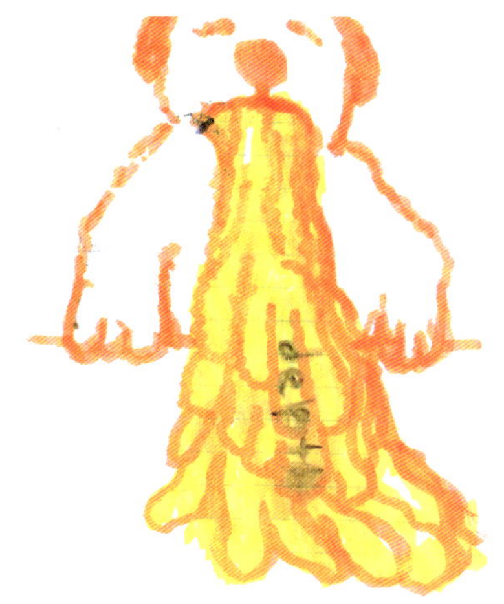
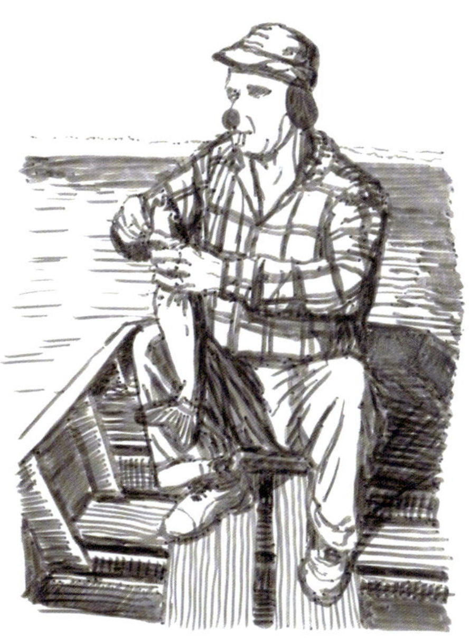
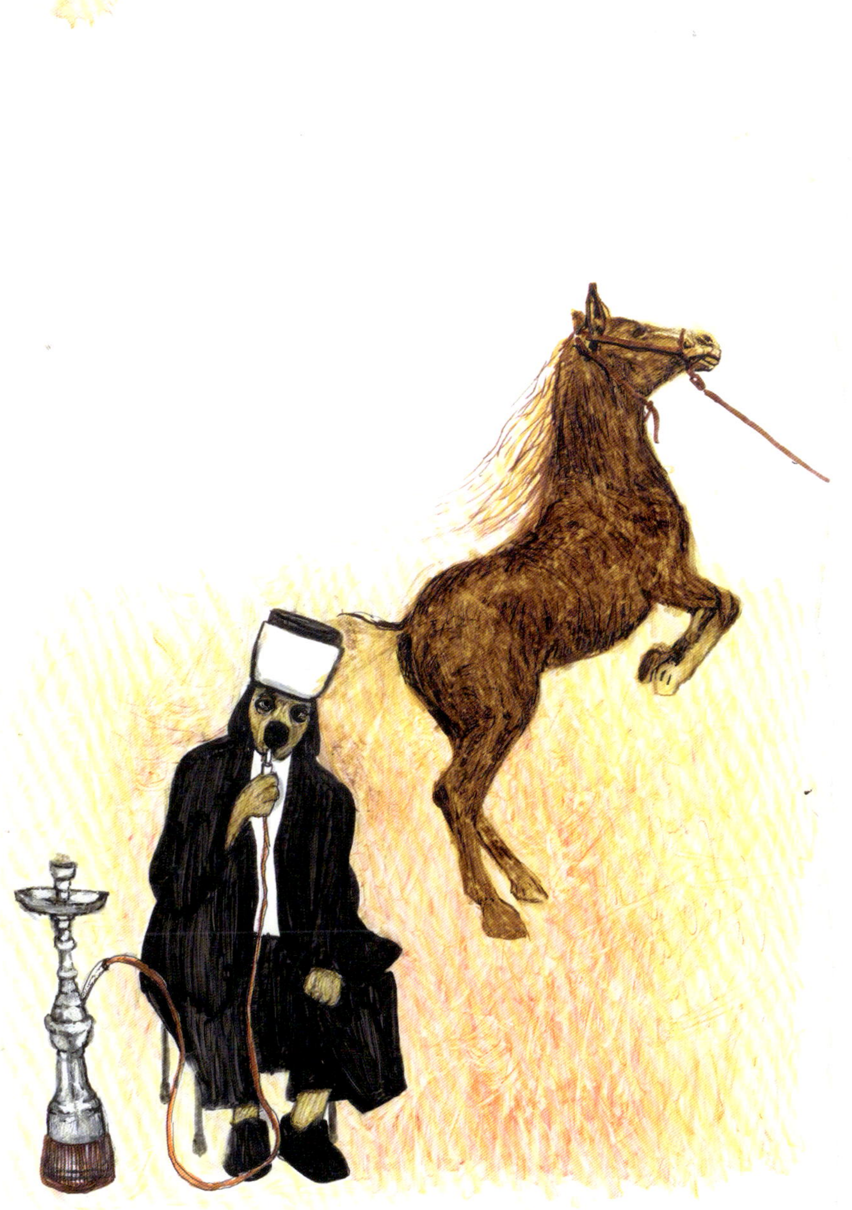

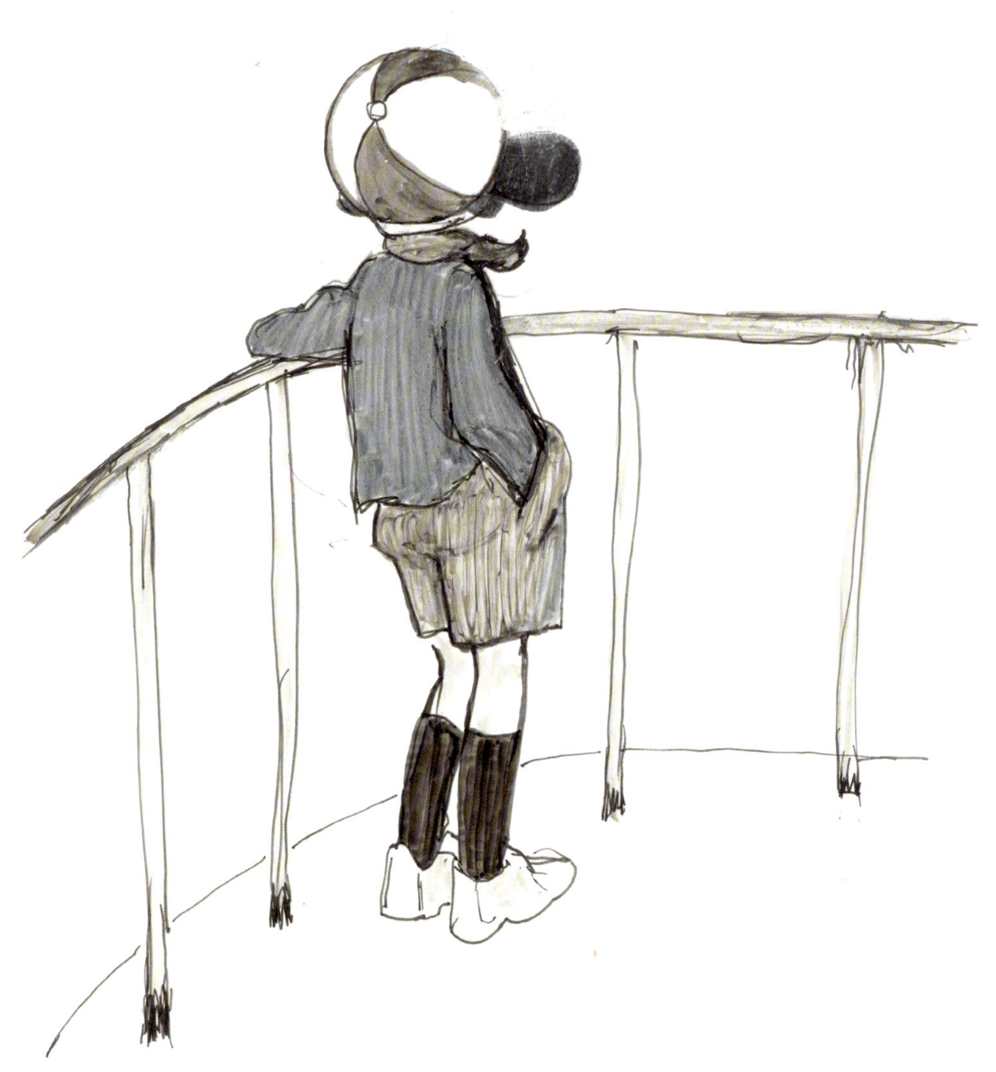

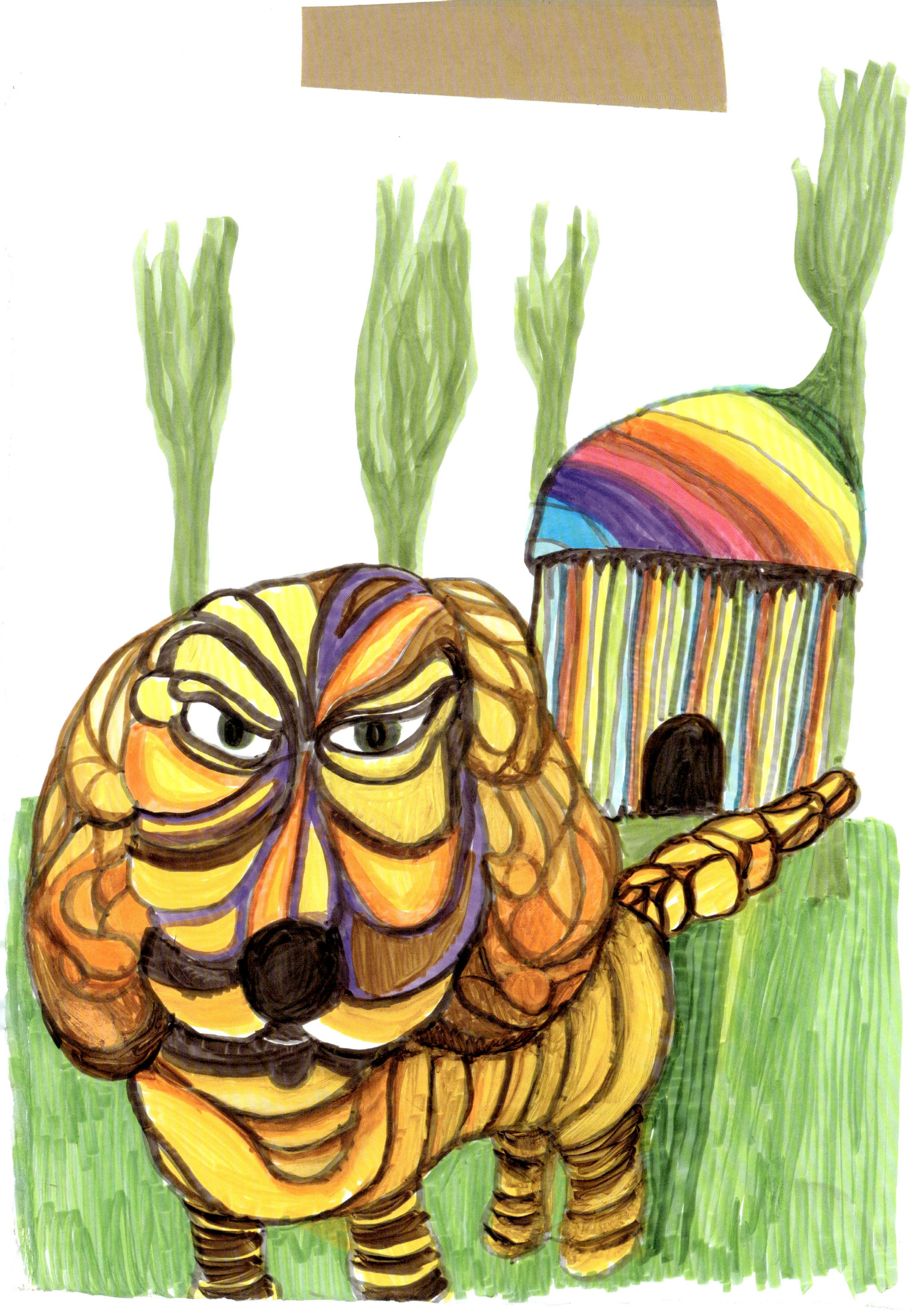

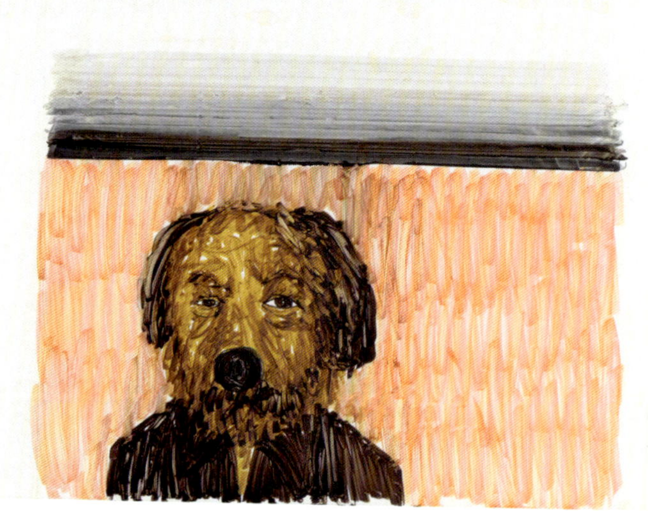

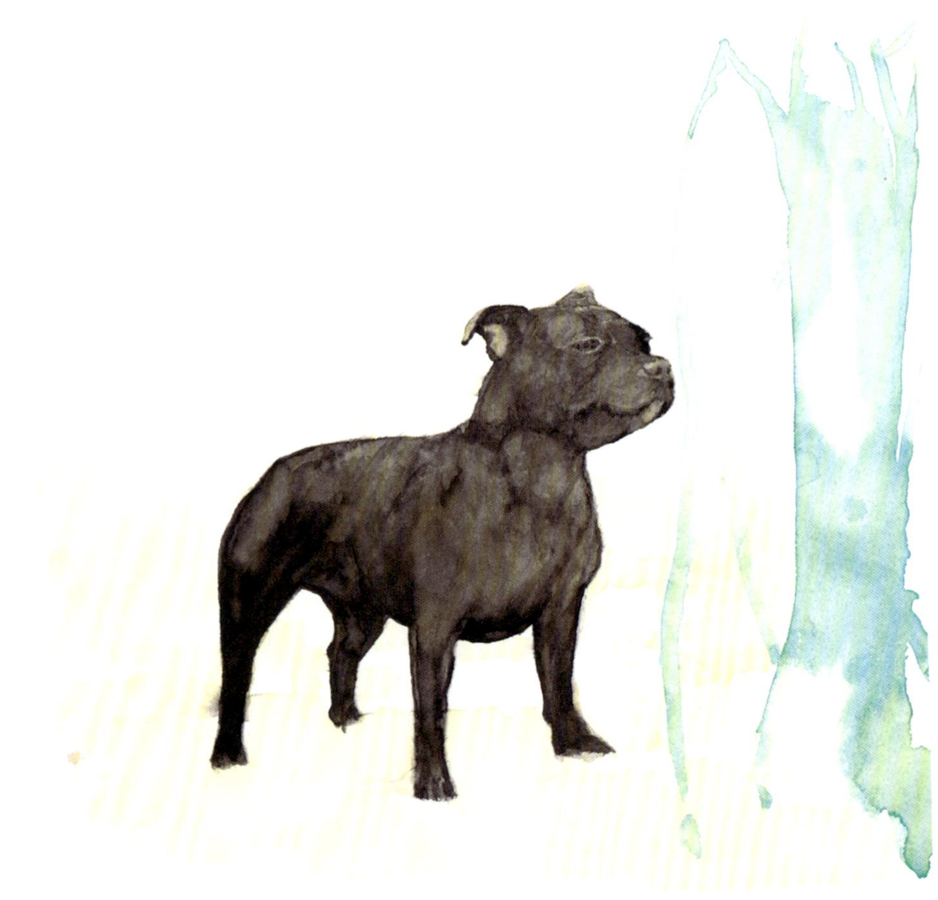

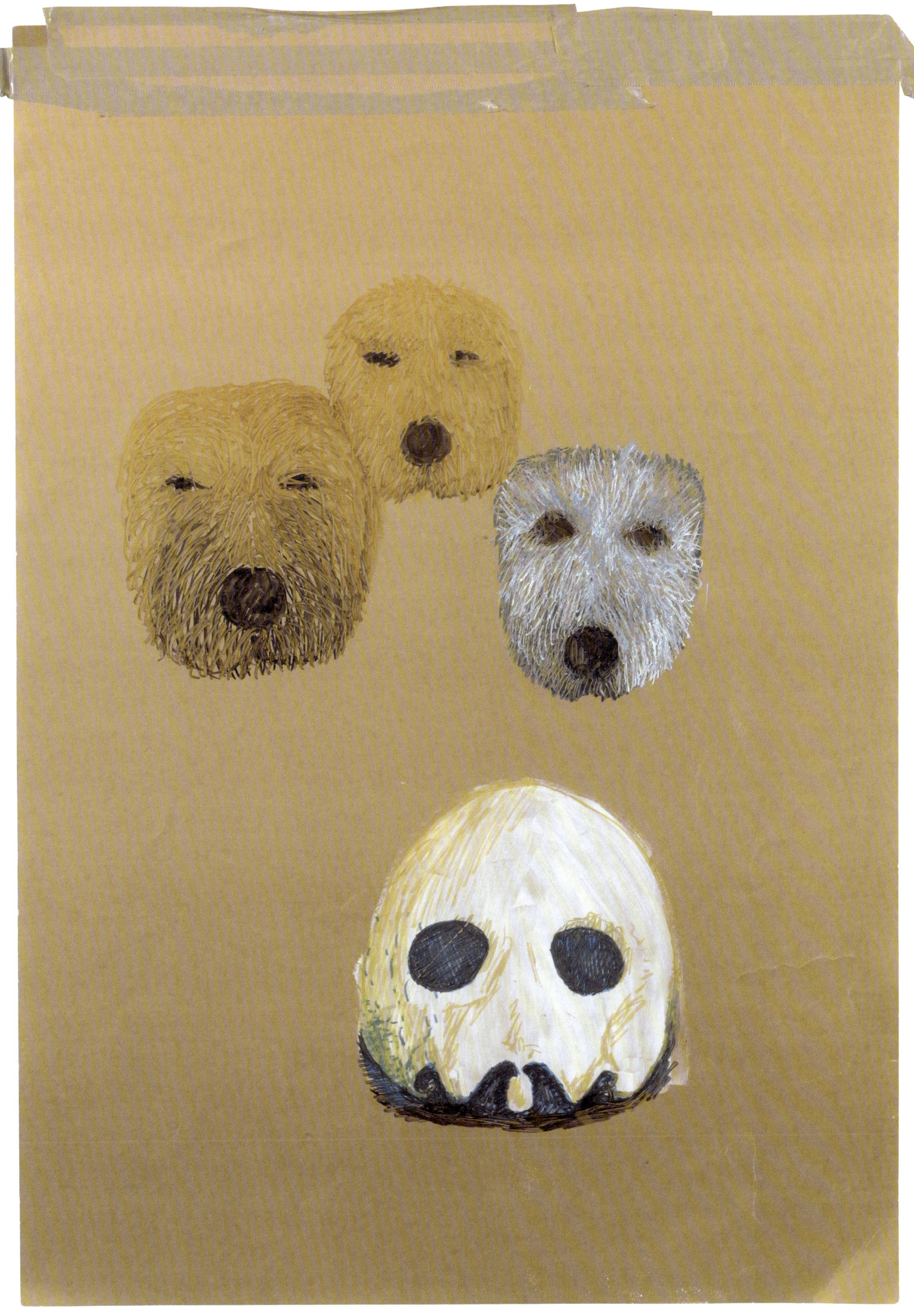

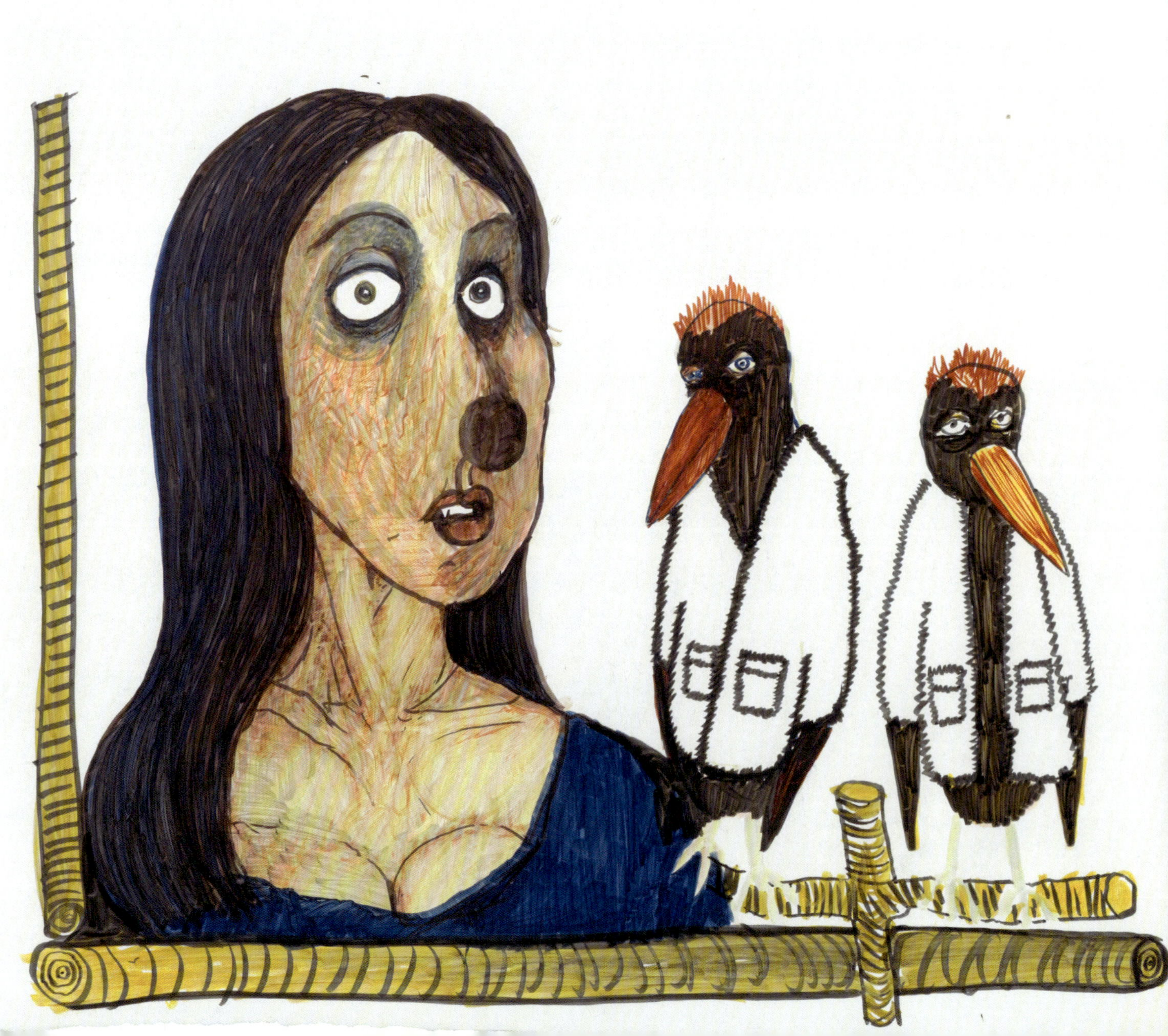

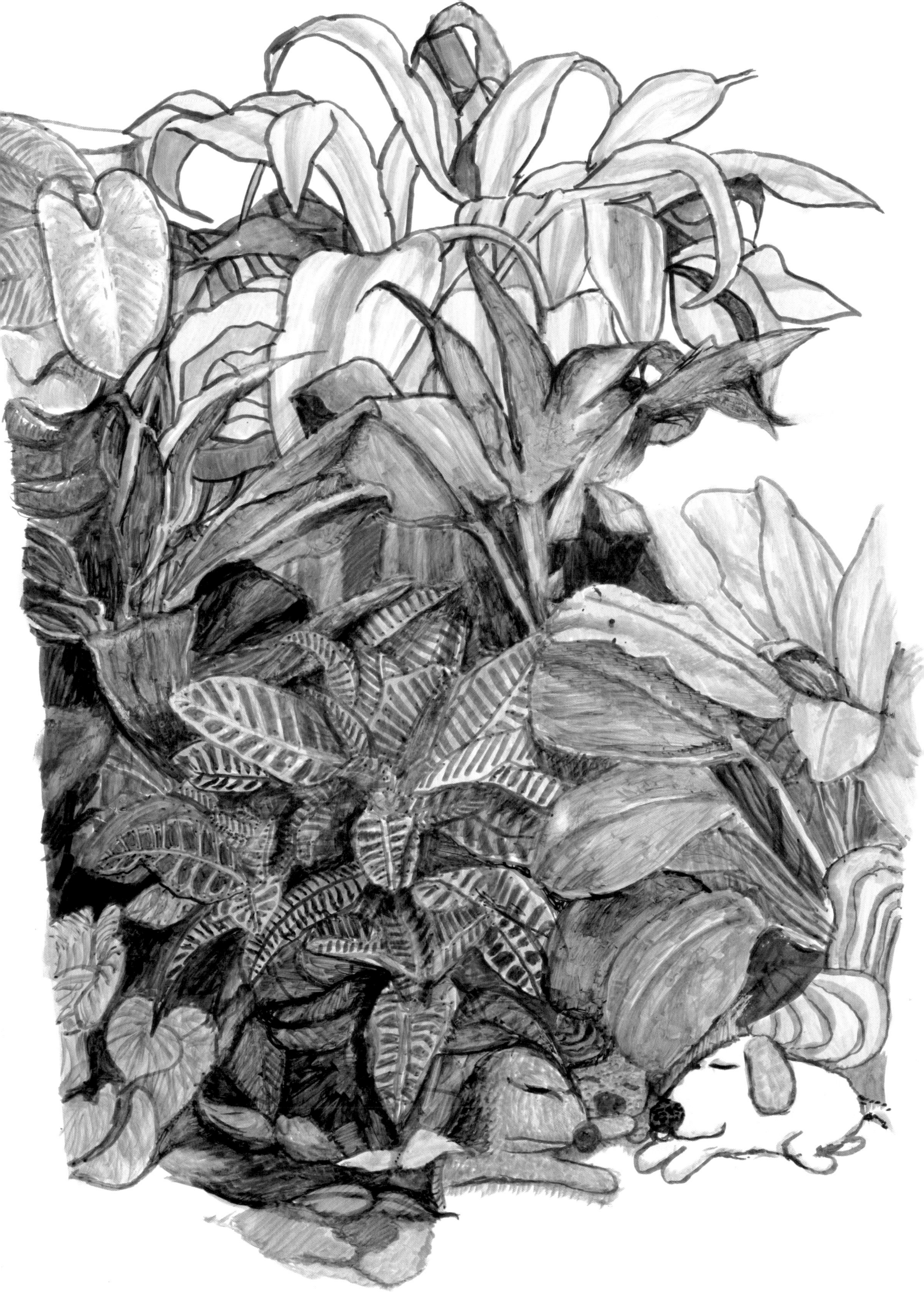

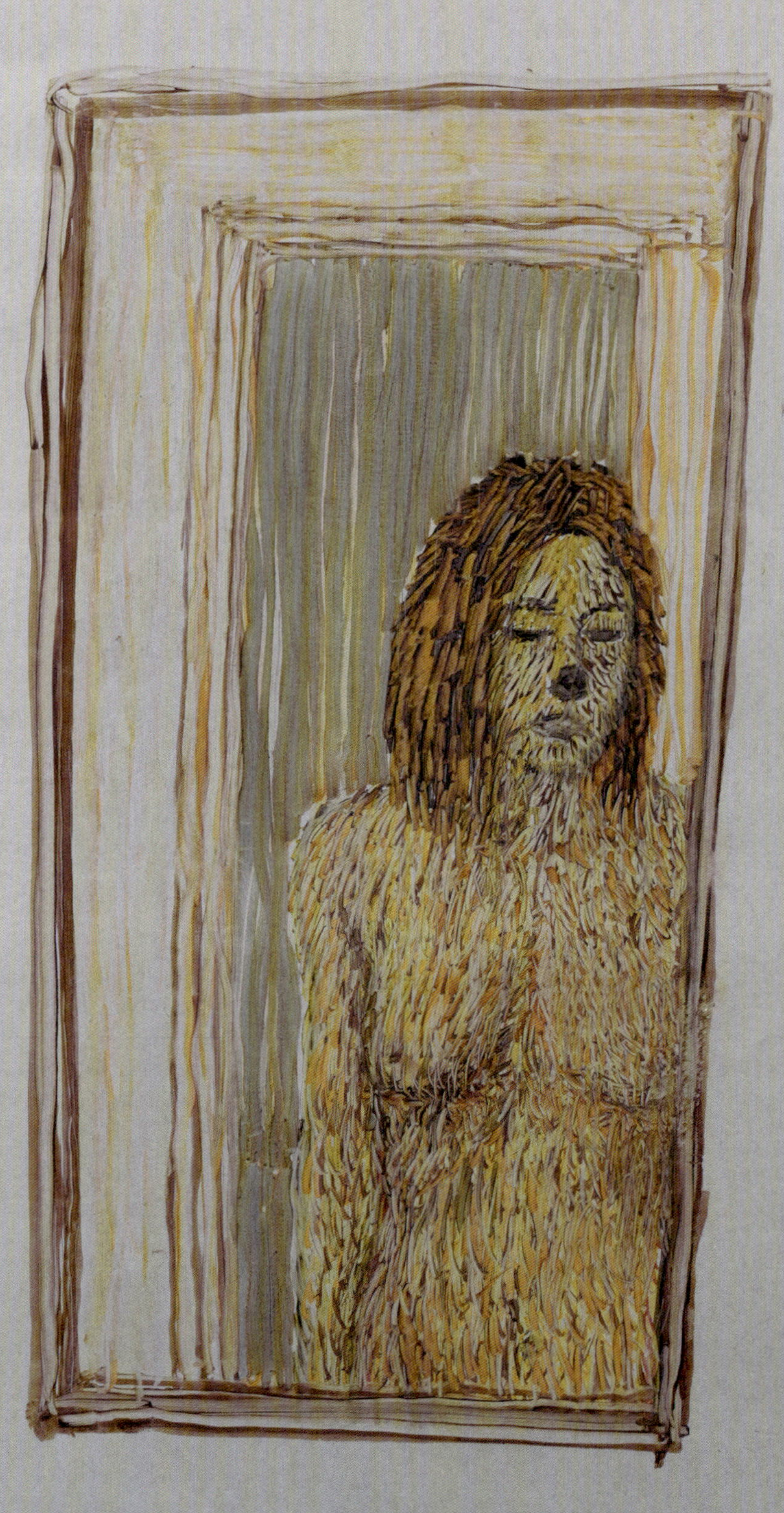

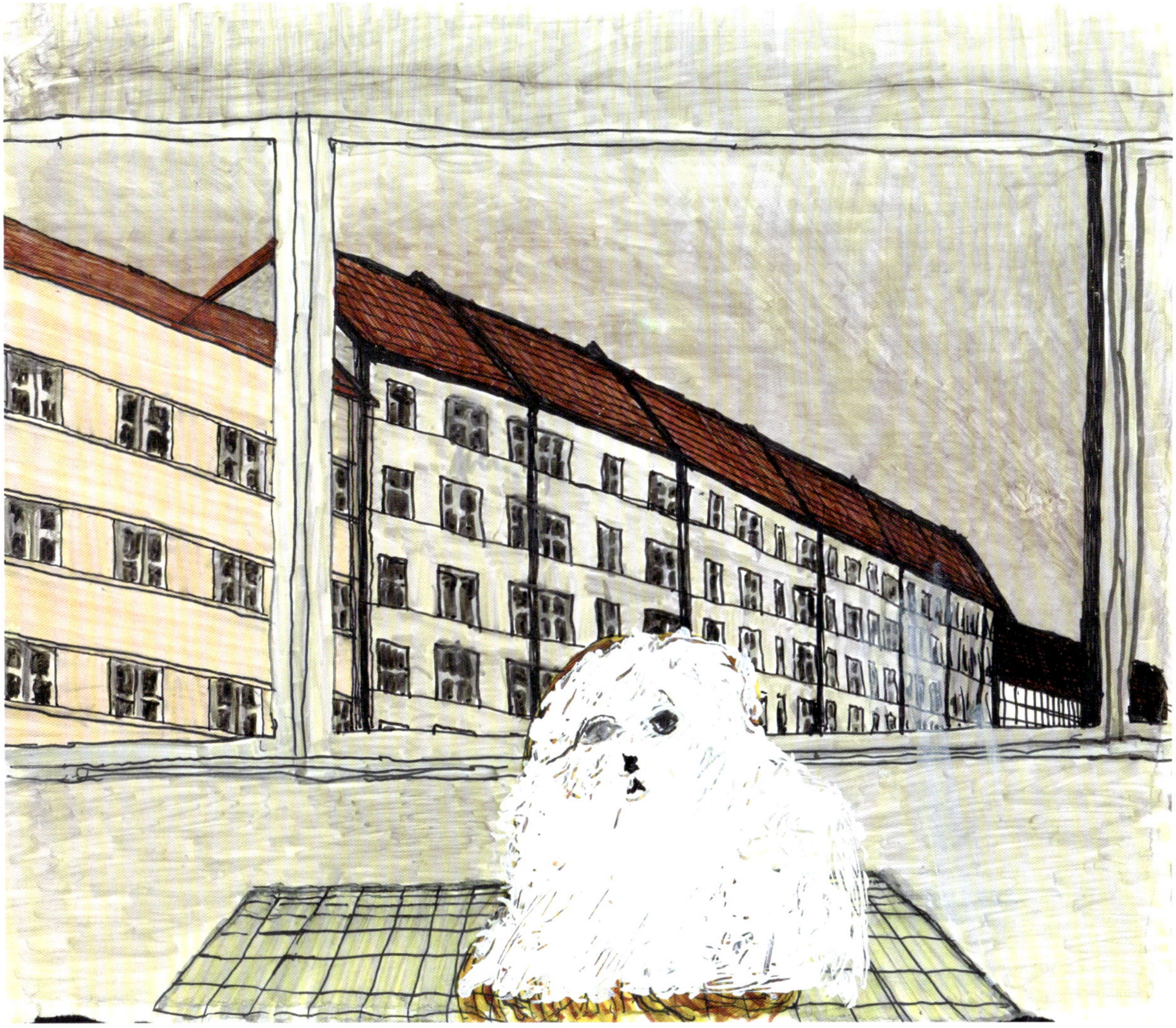

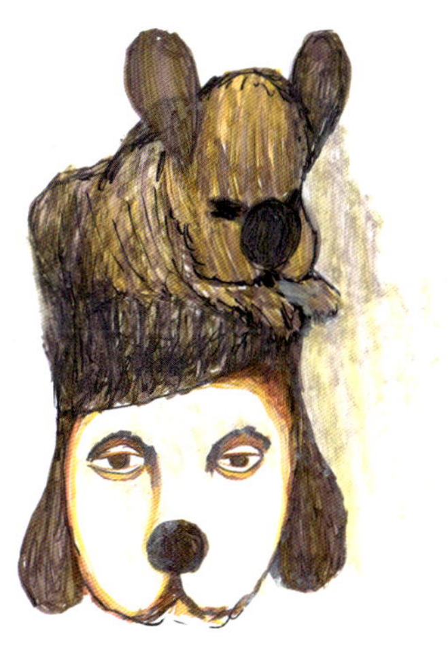

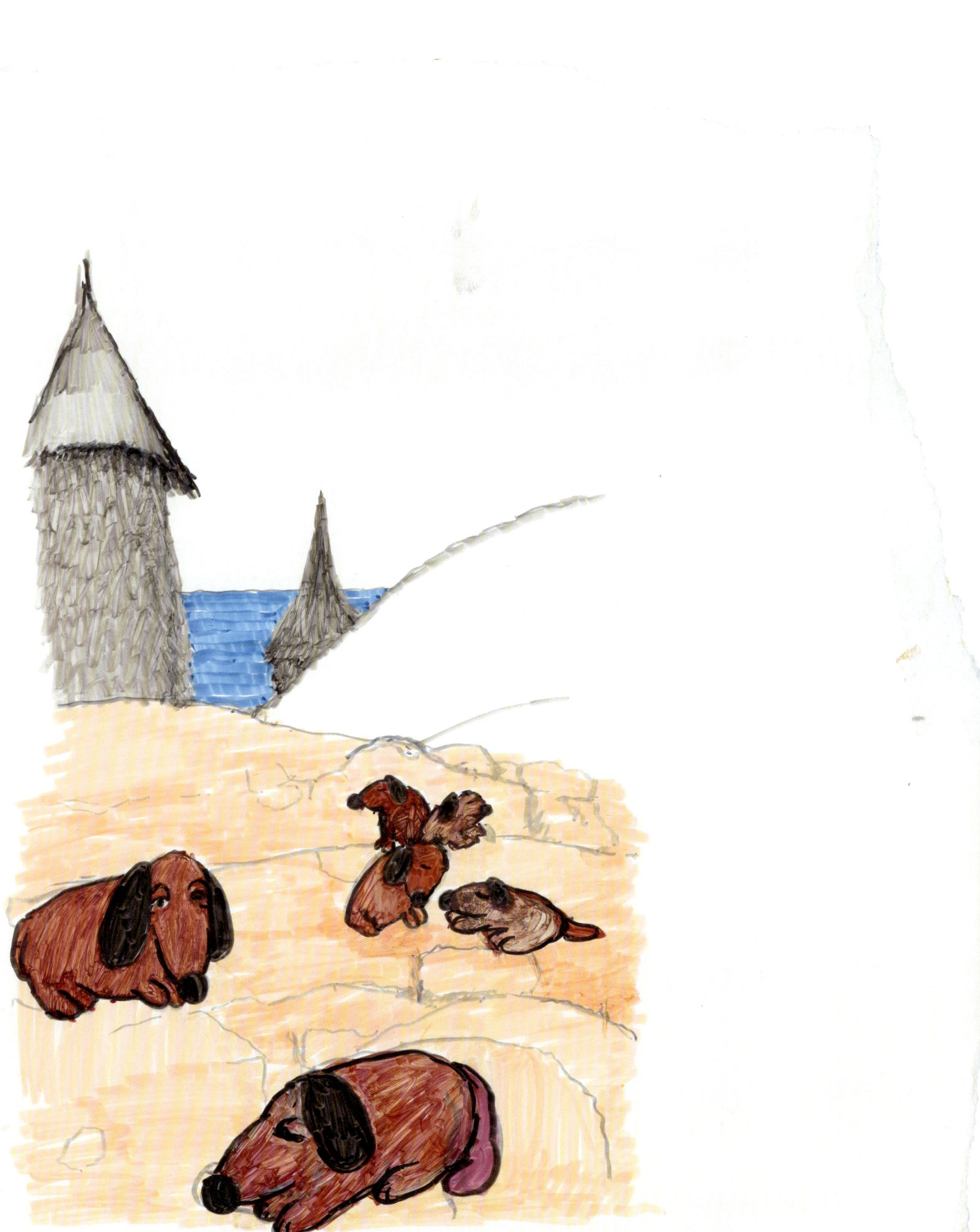

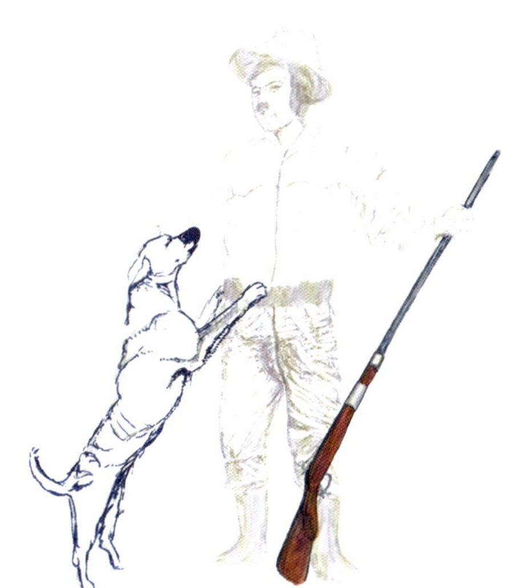
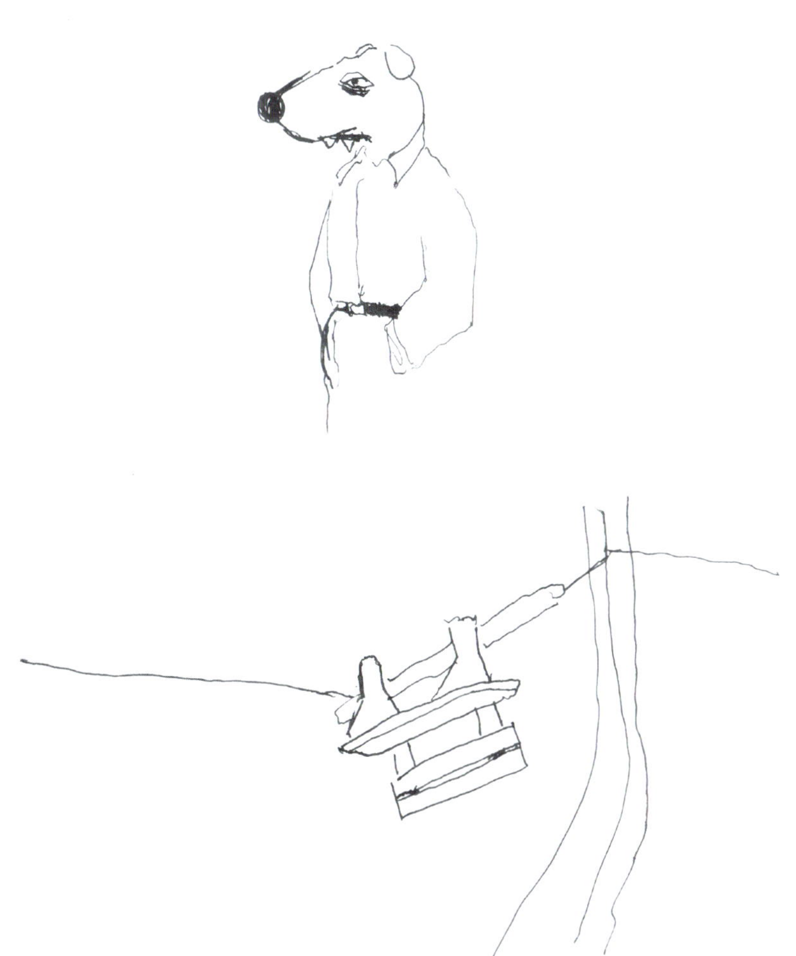

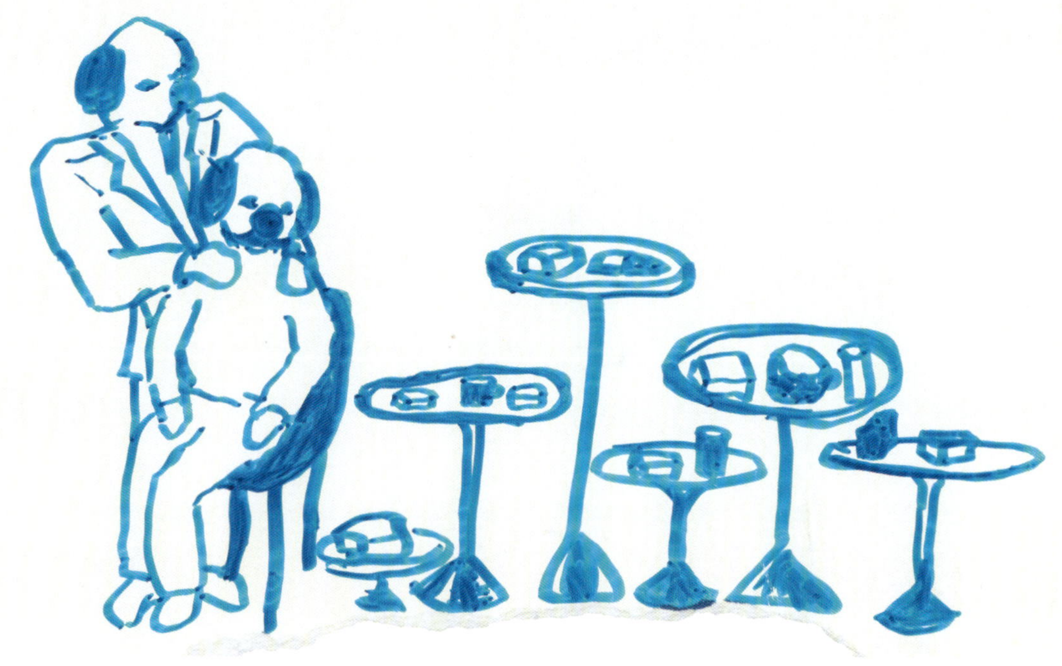

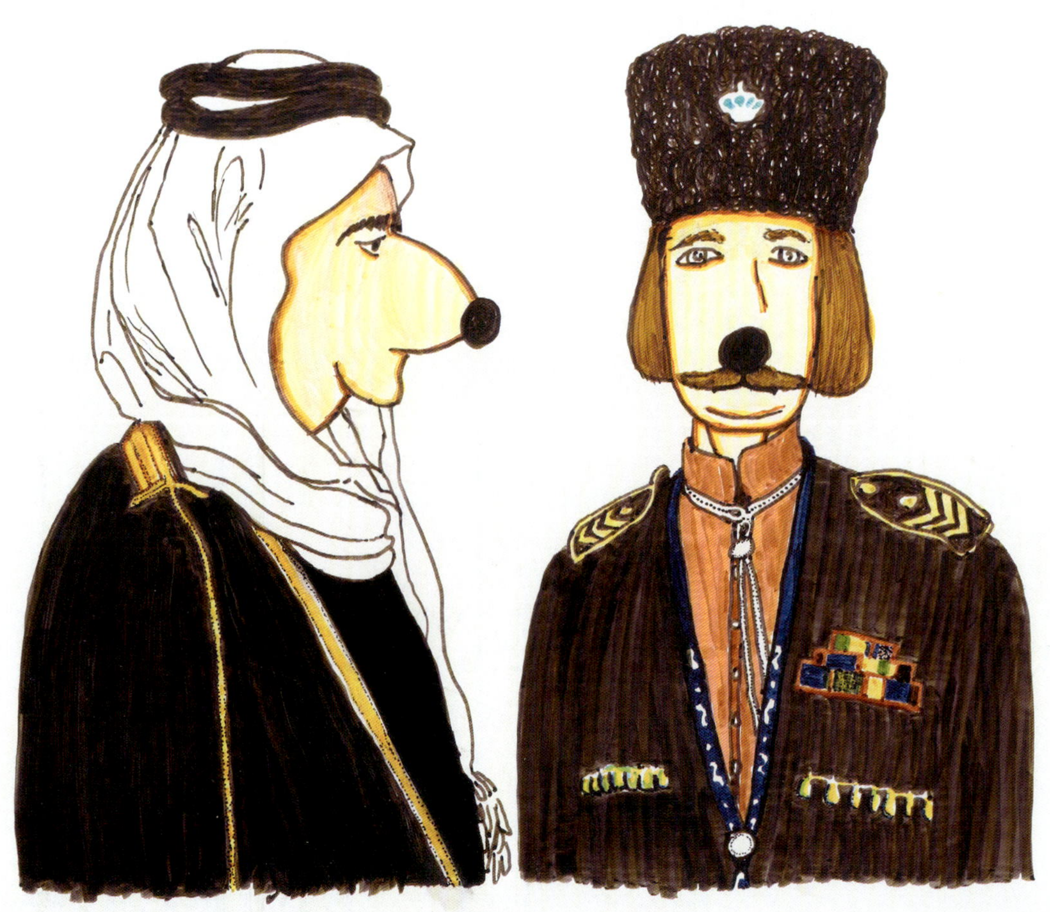

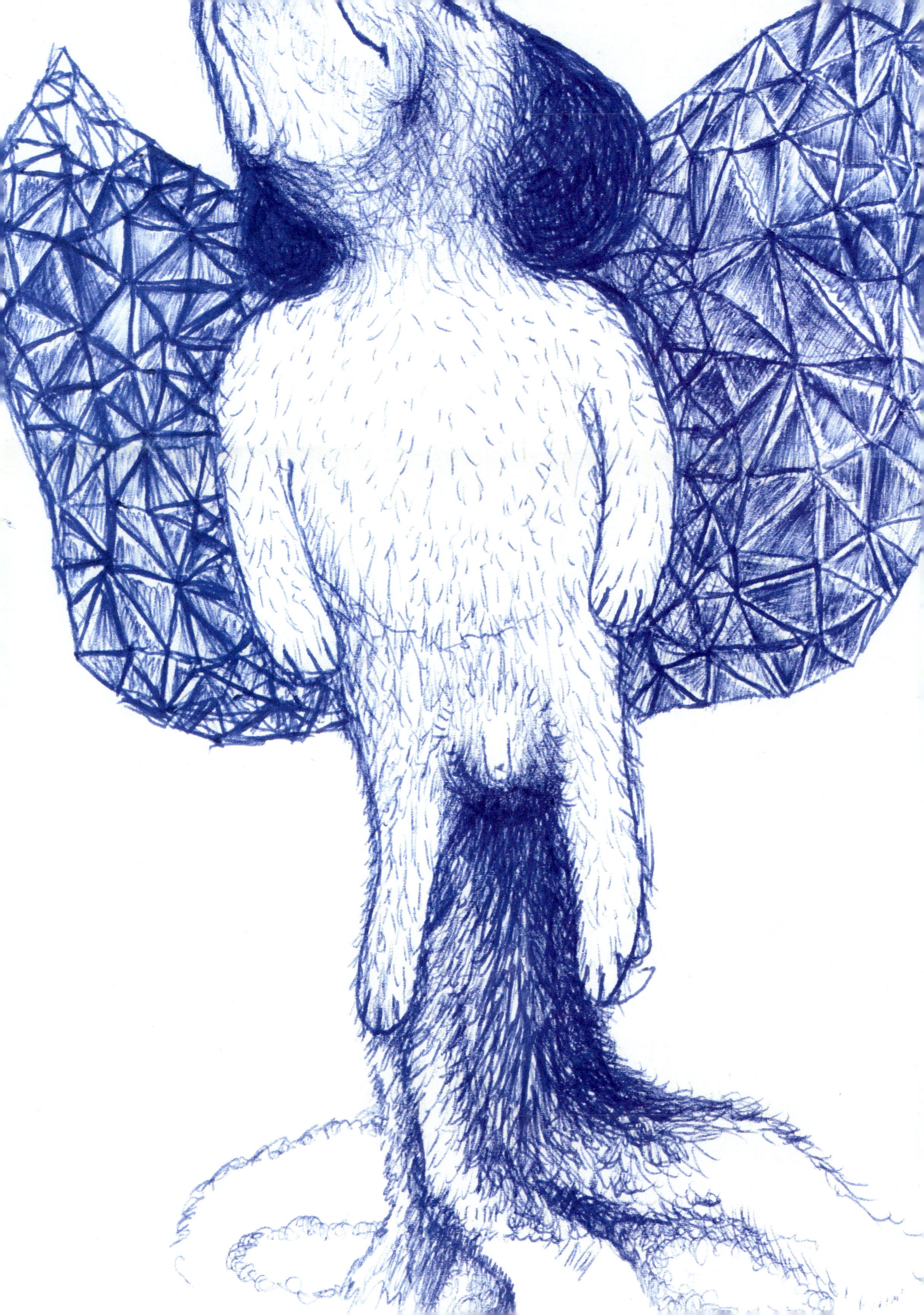

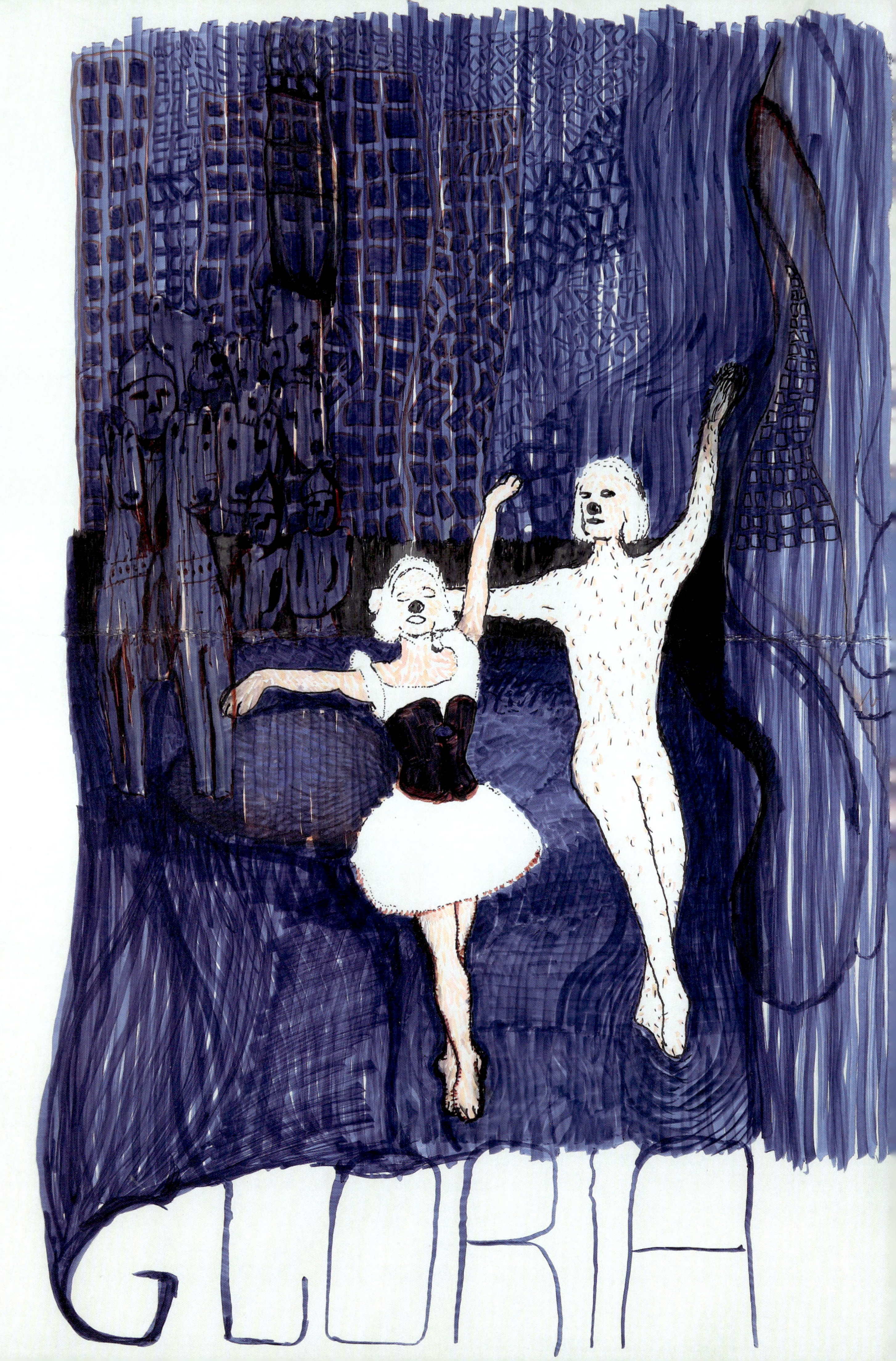

GLORIA

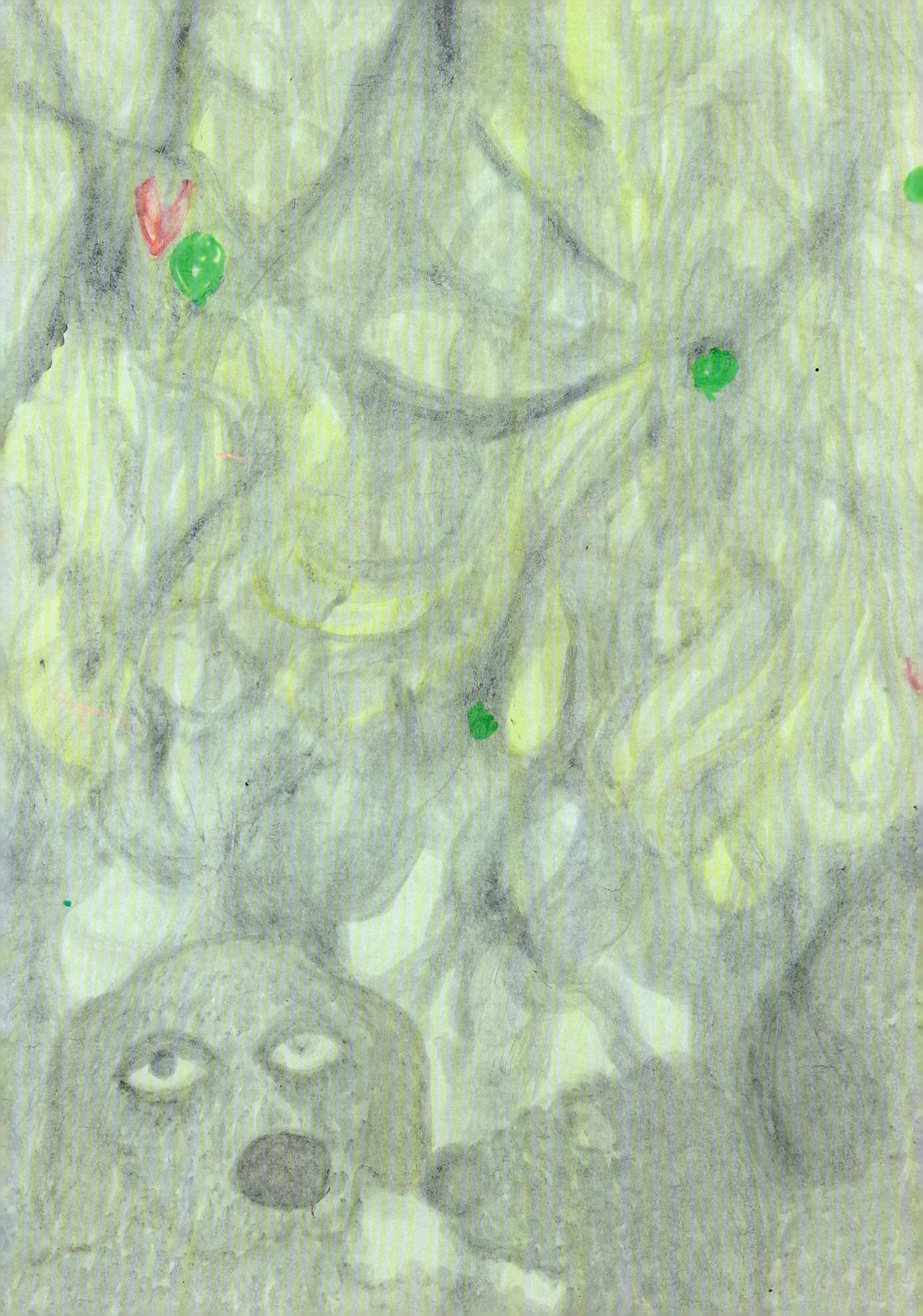

FANTA

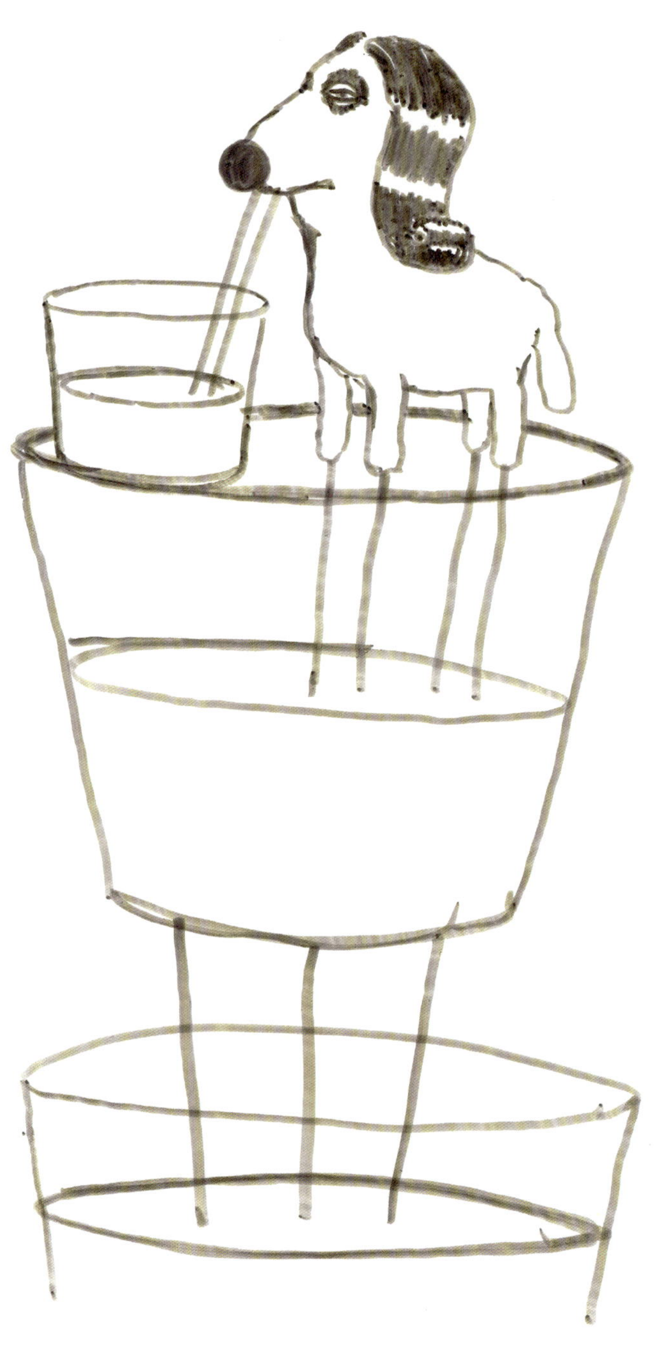

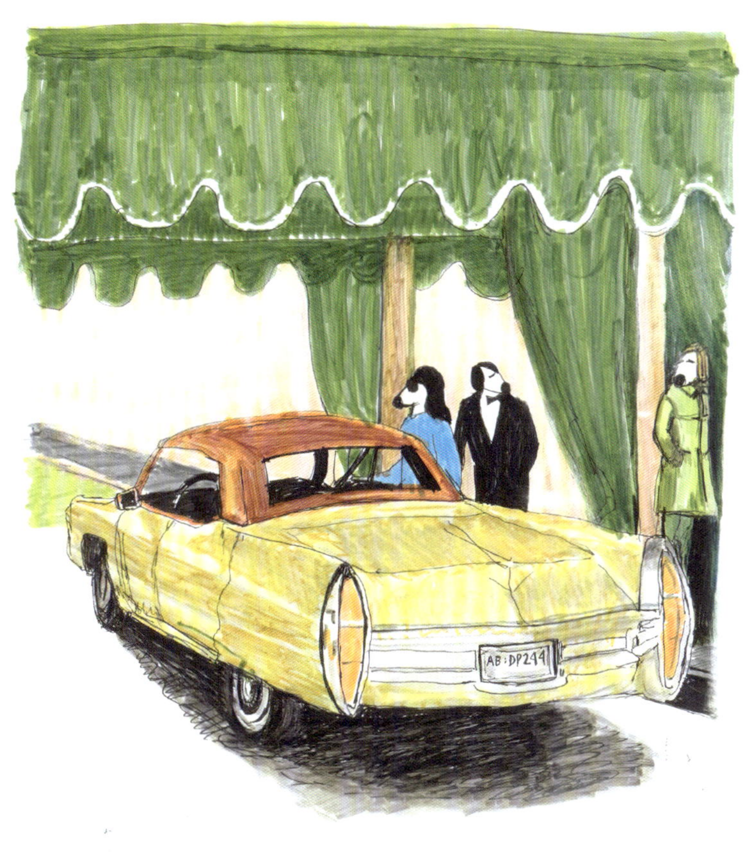

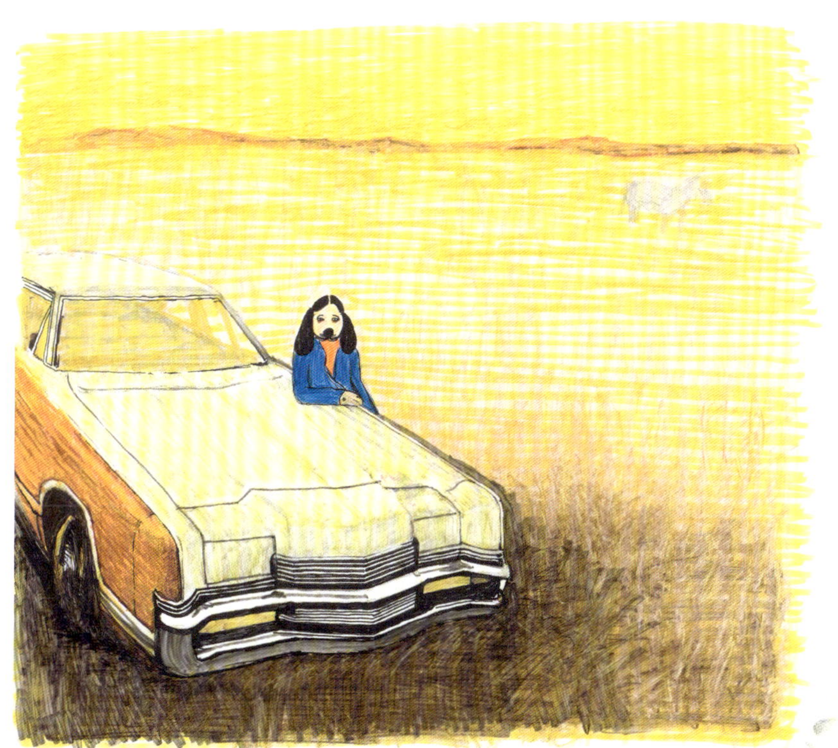

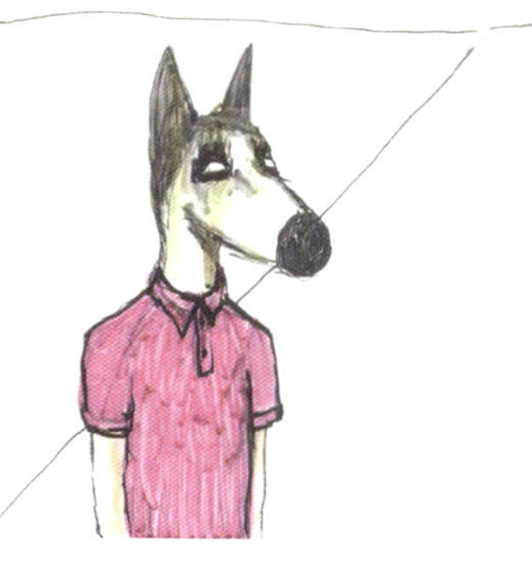

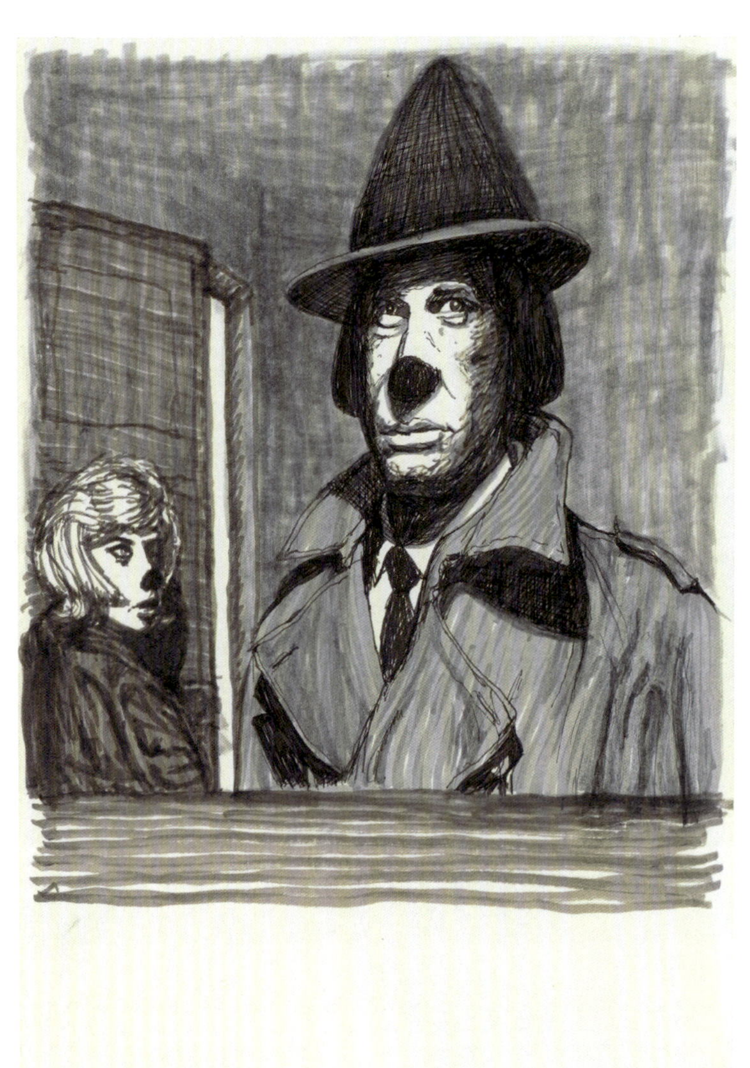

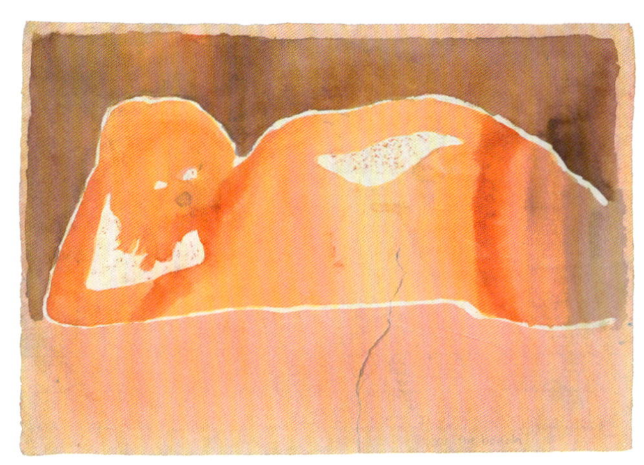

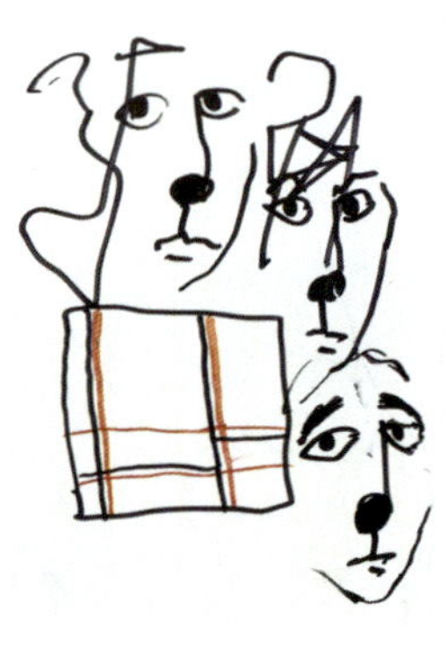

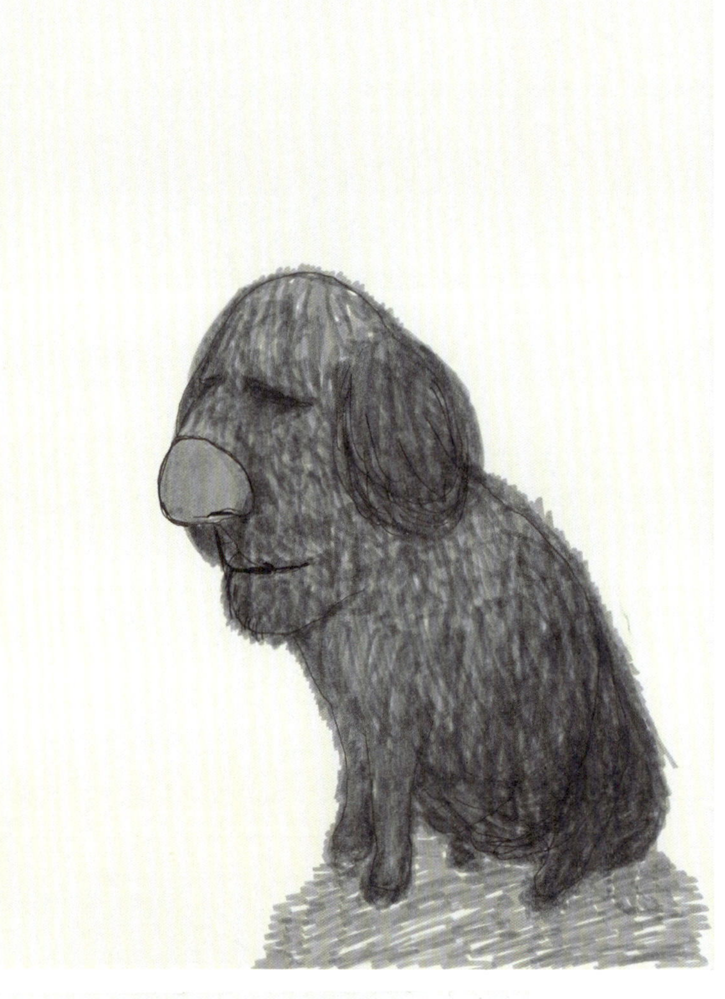

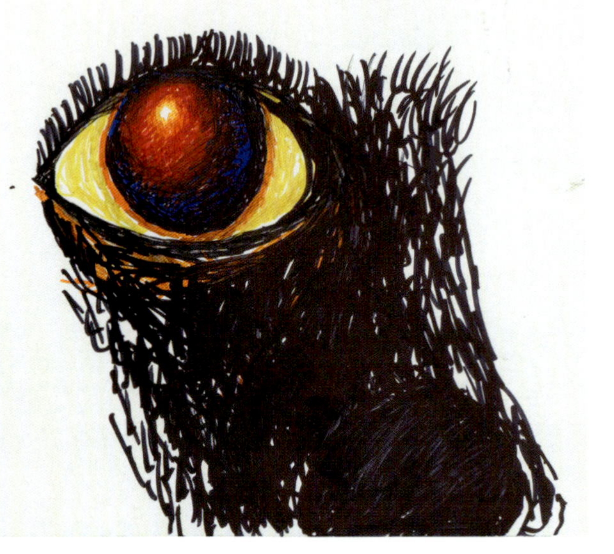

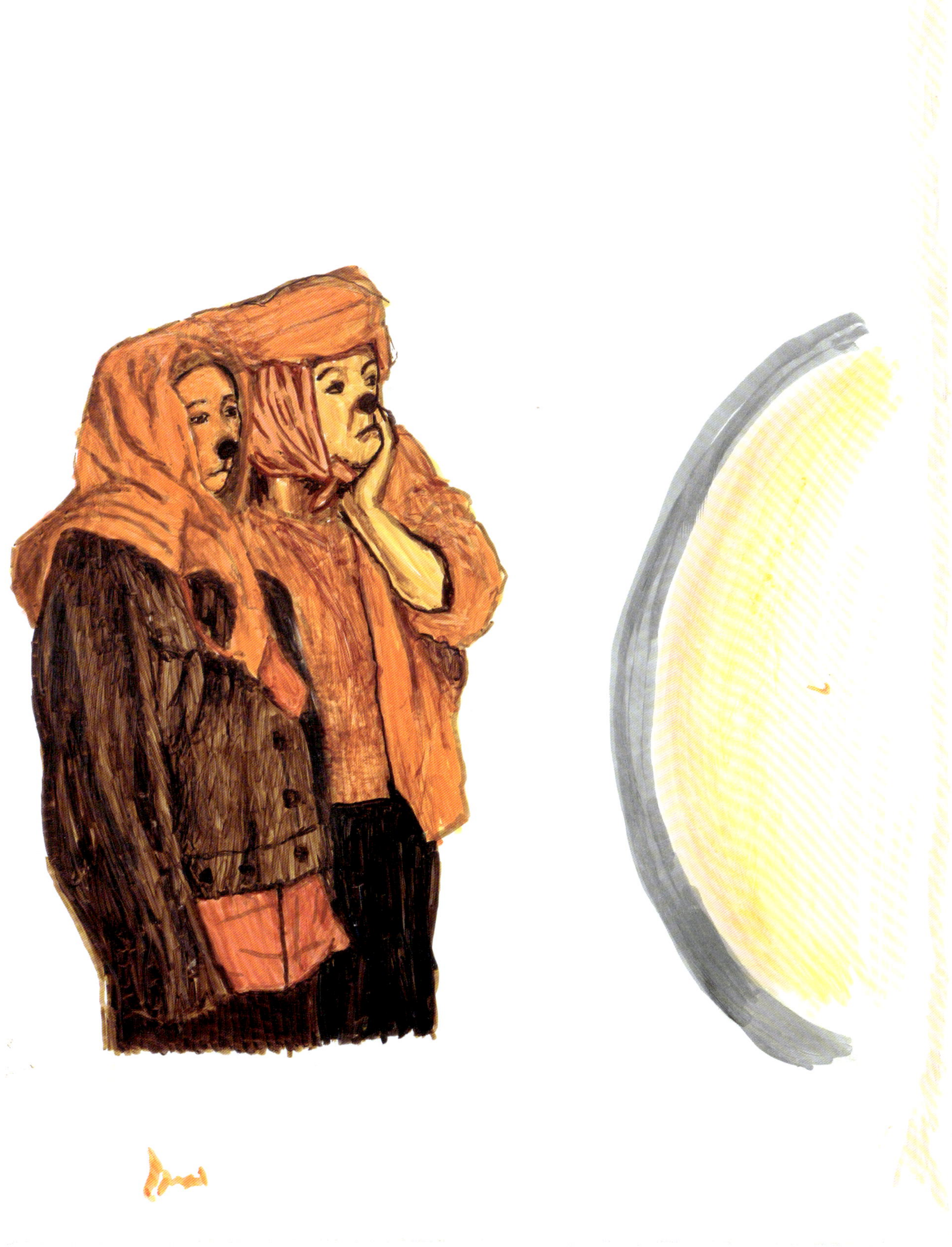

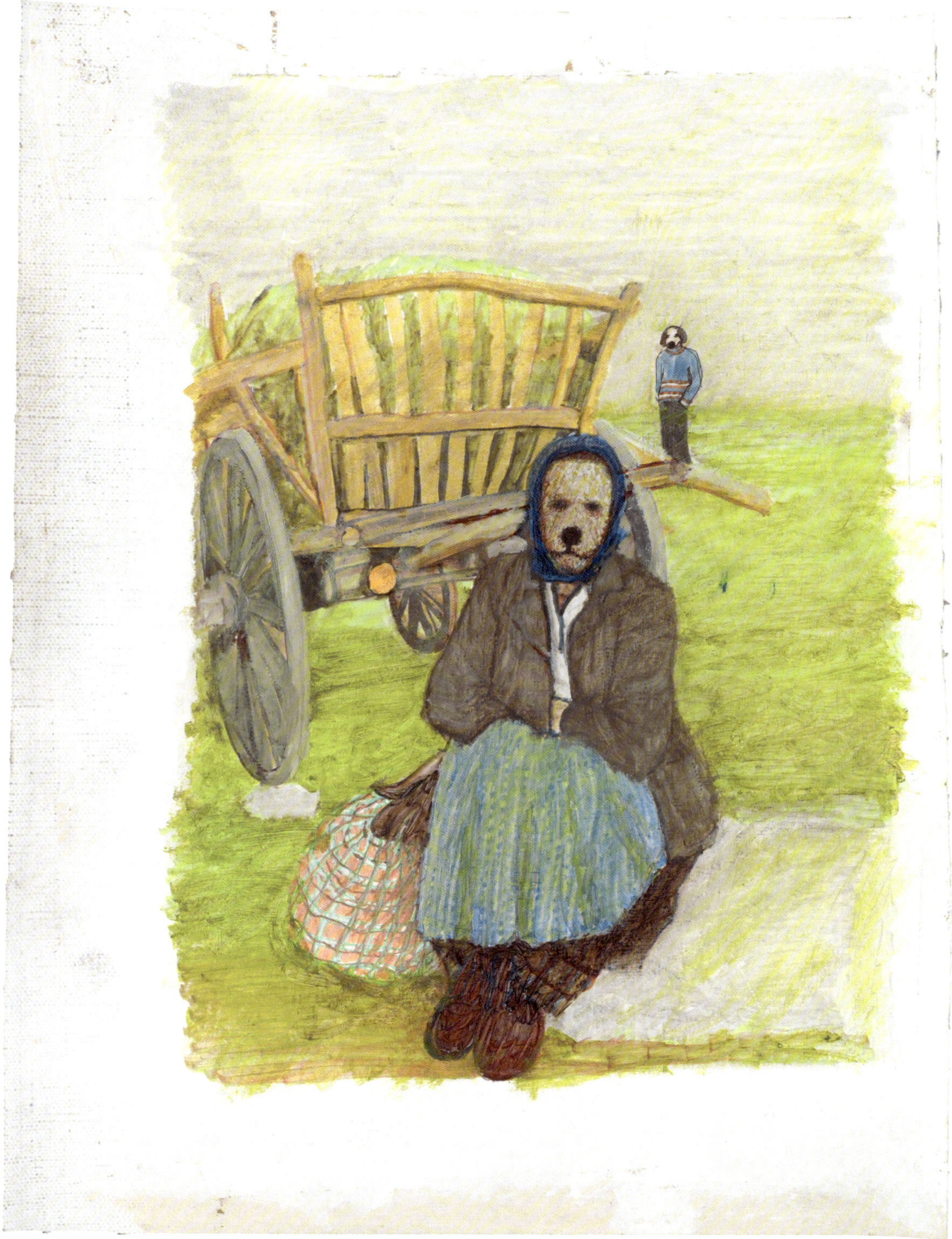

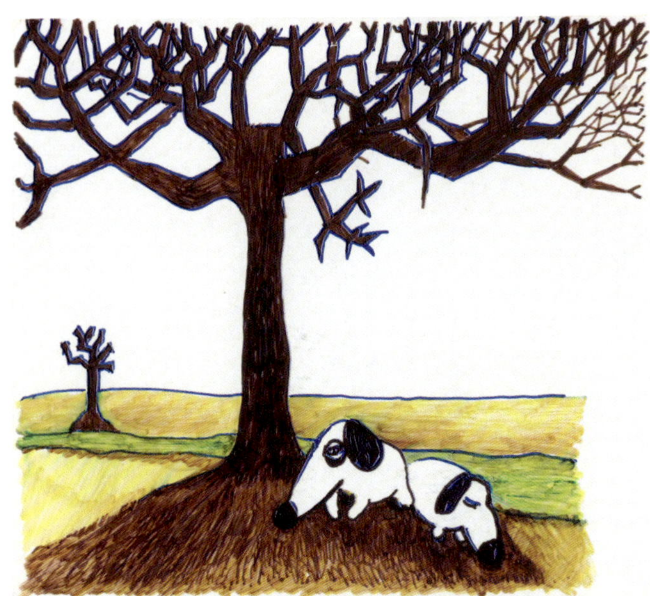

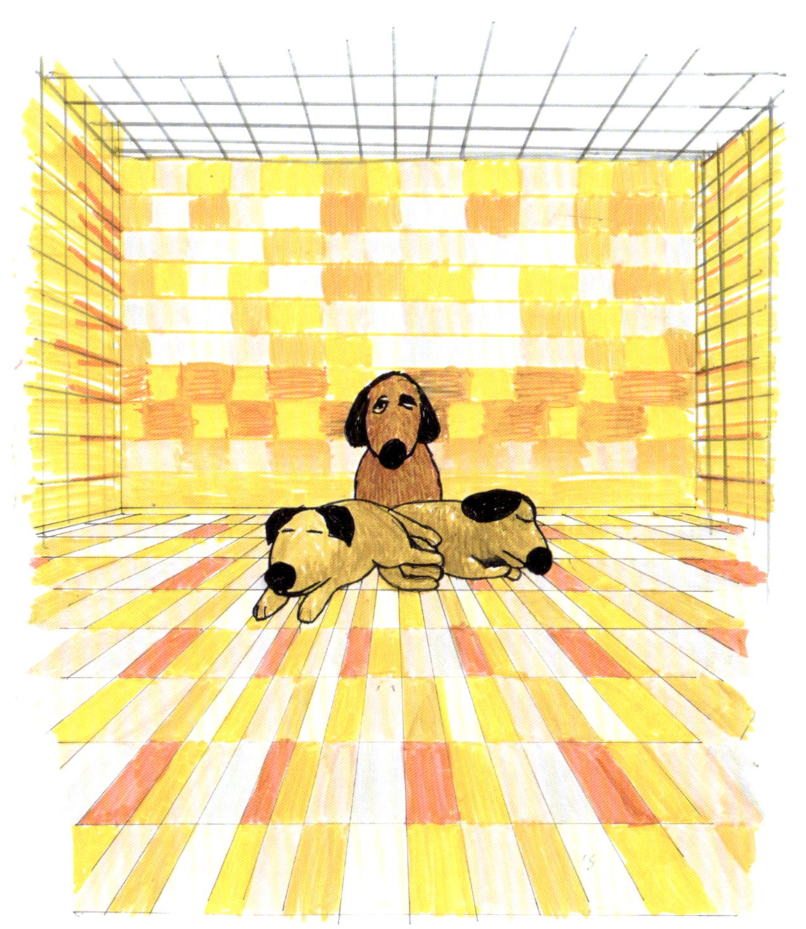

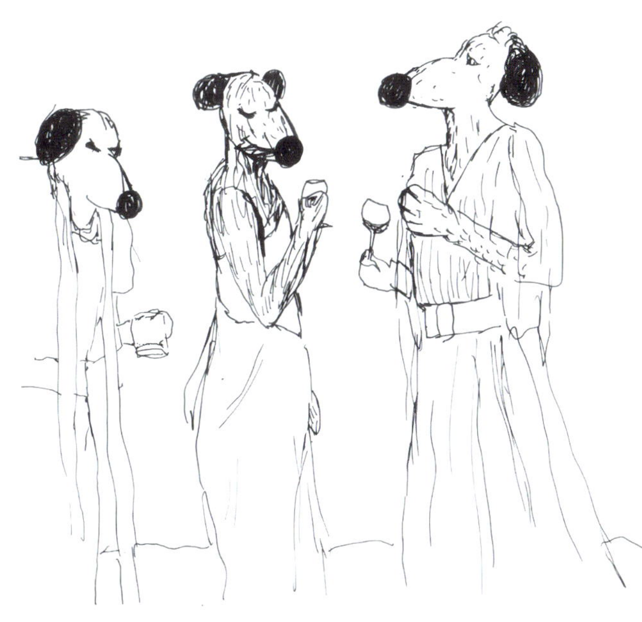

Honig
Rome II   Sergej
Kaffemühle   Sergej
Rotwein   S
Brot
Bananen
Frühlingszw.
Führerschein
Bibel in gerechter Sprache

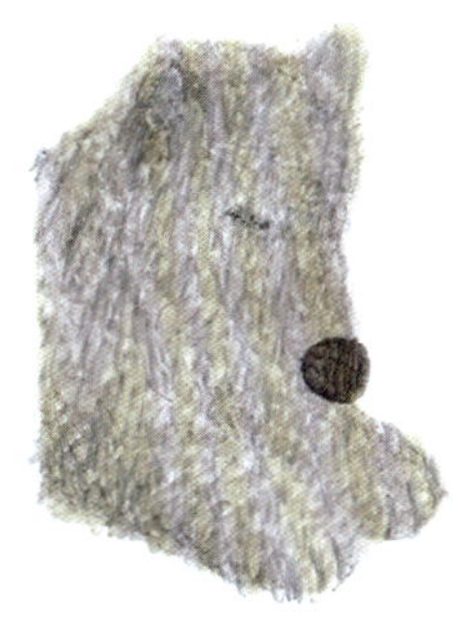

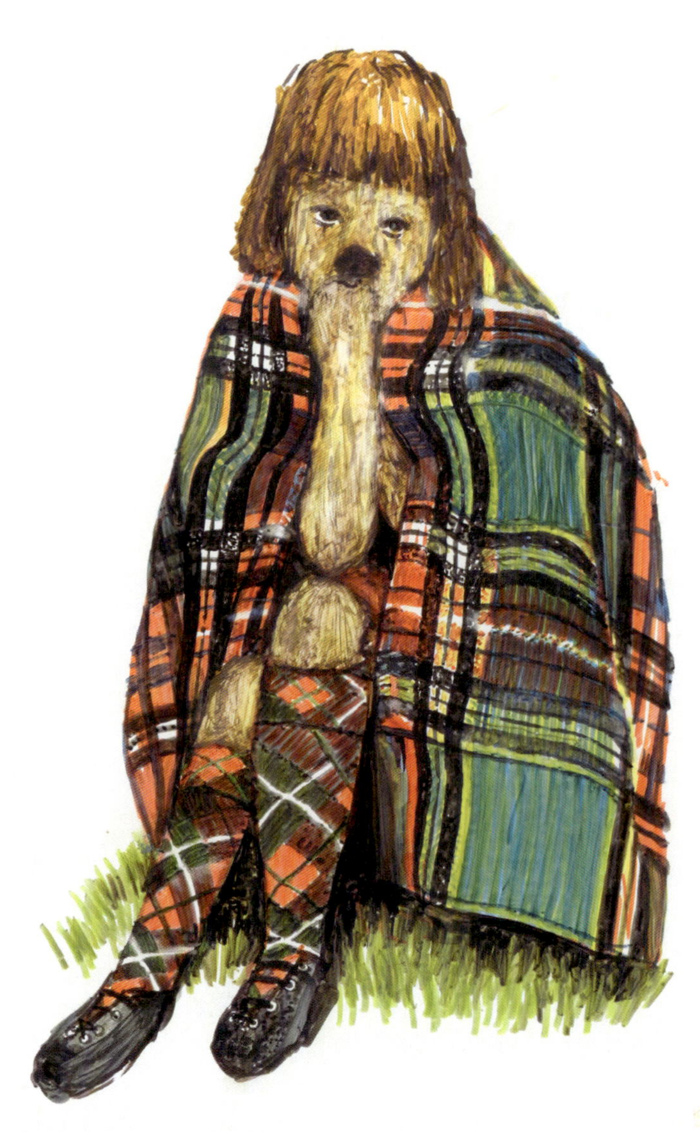

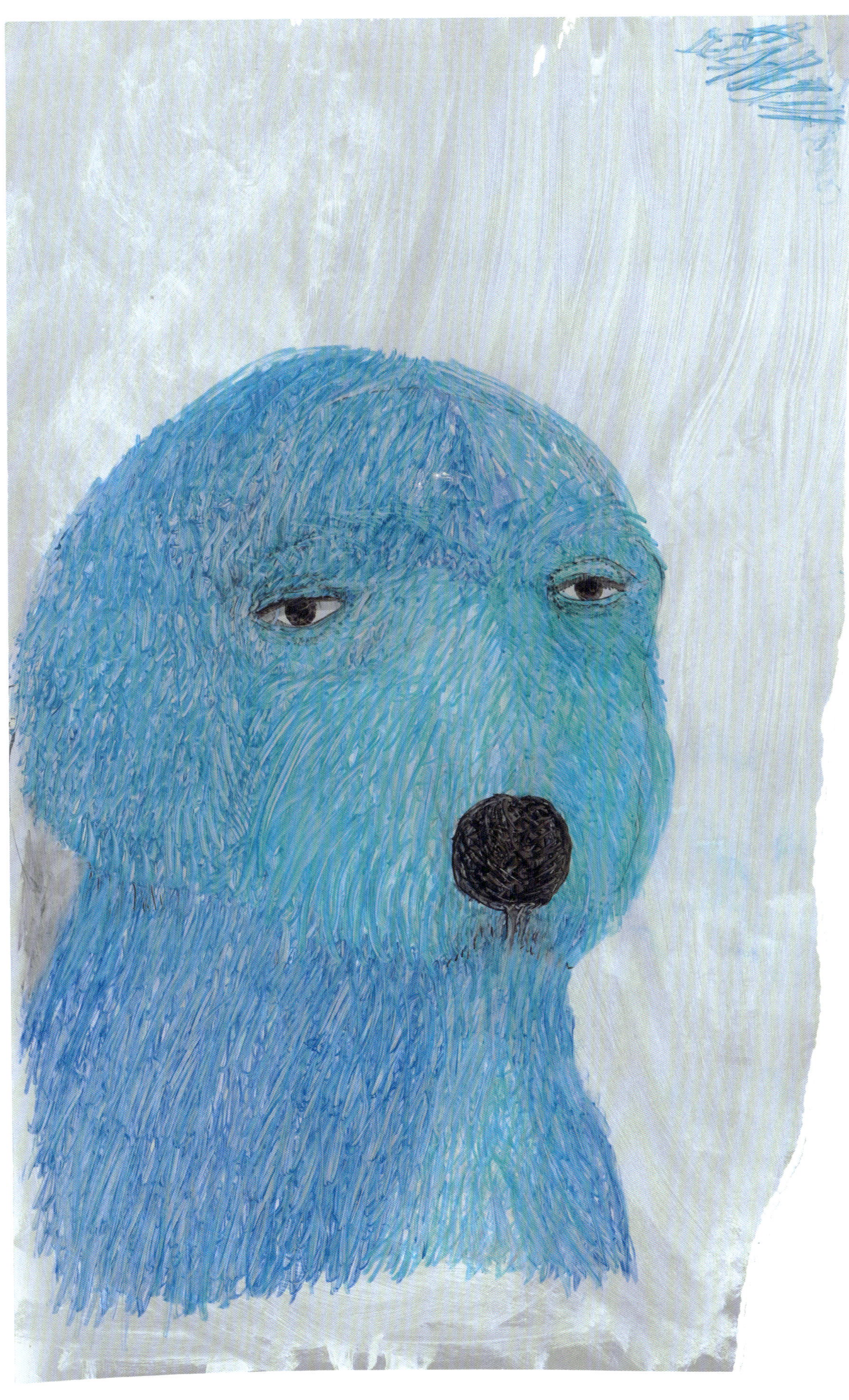

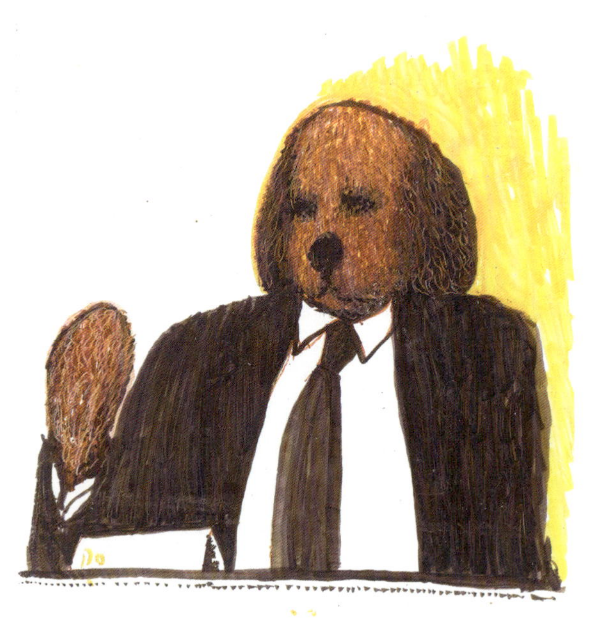

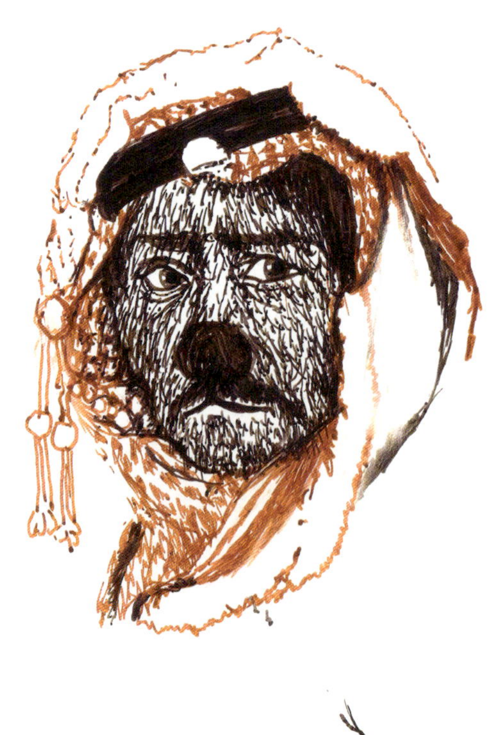

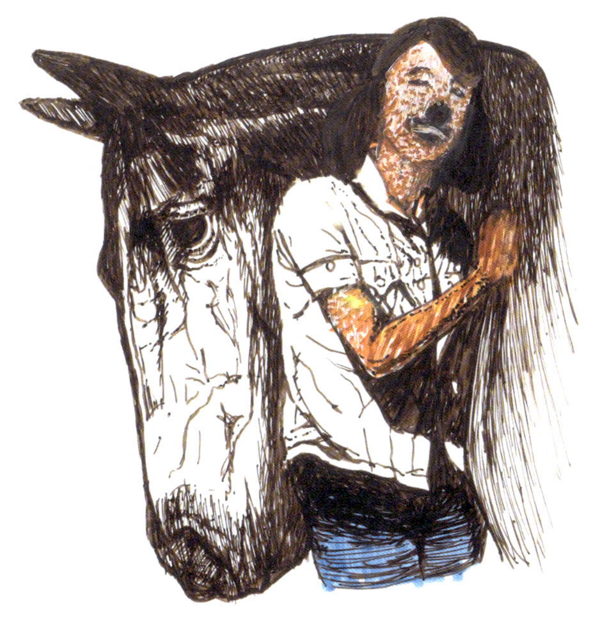

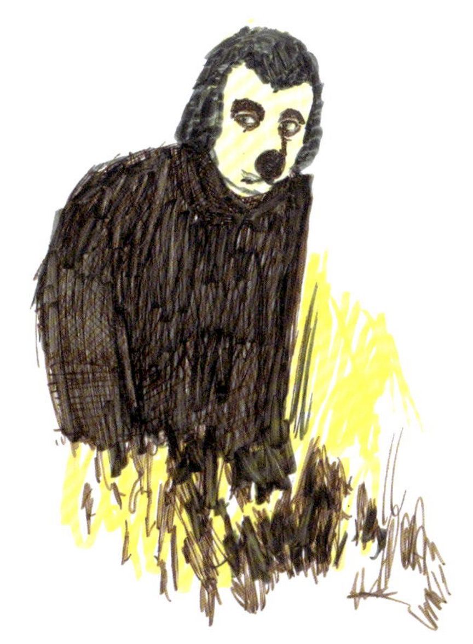

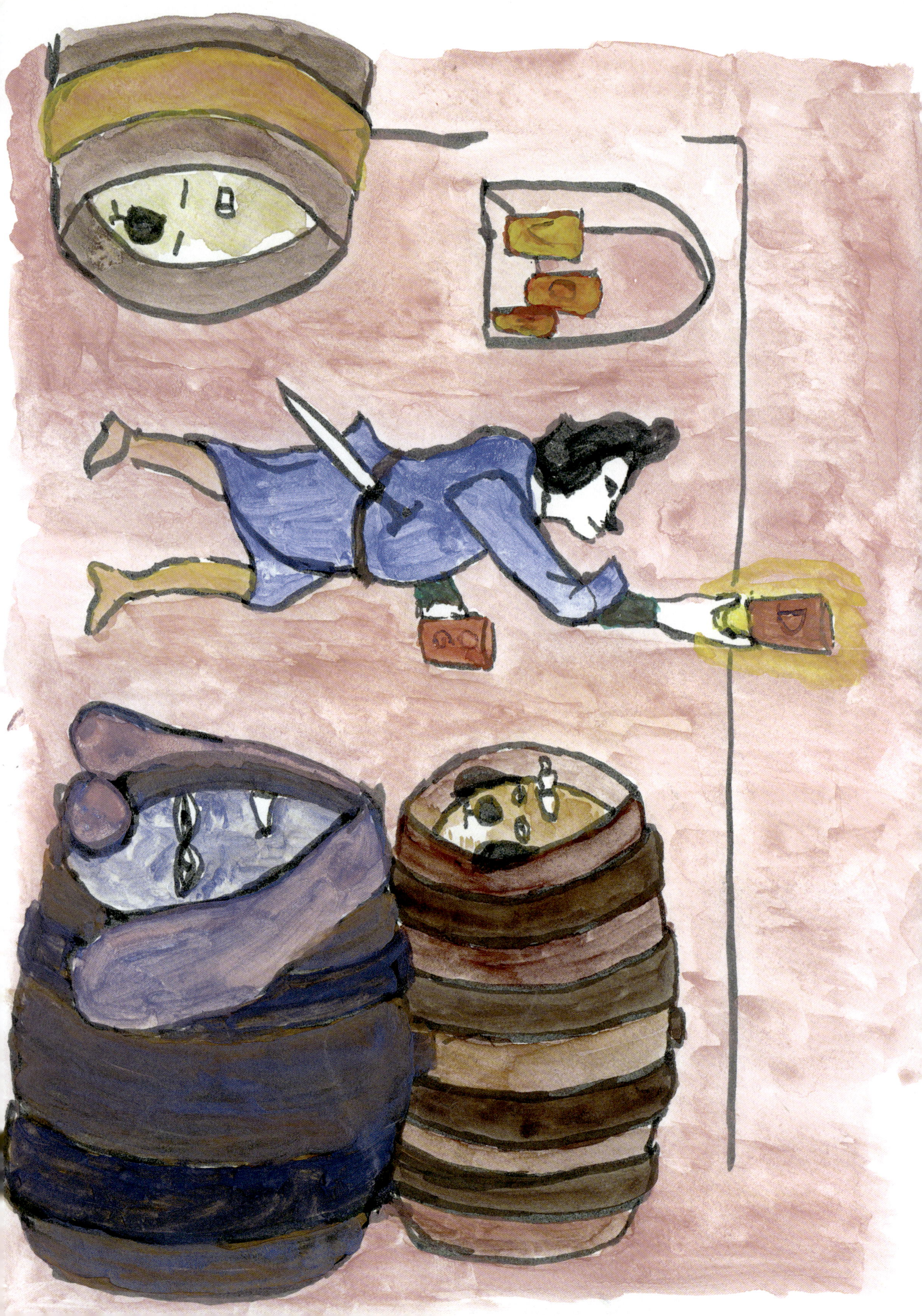

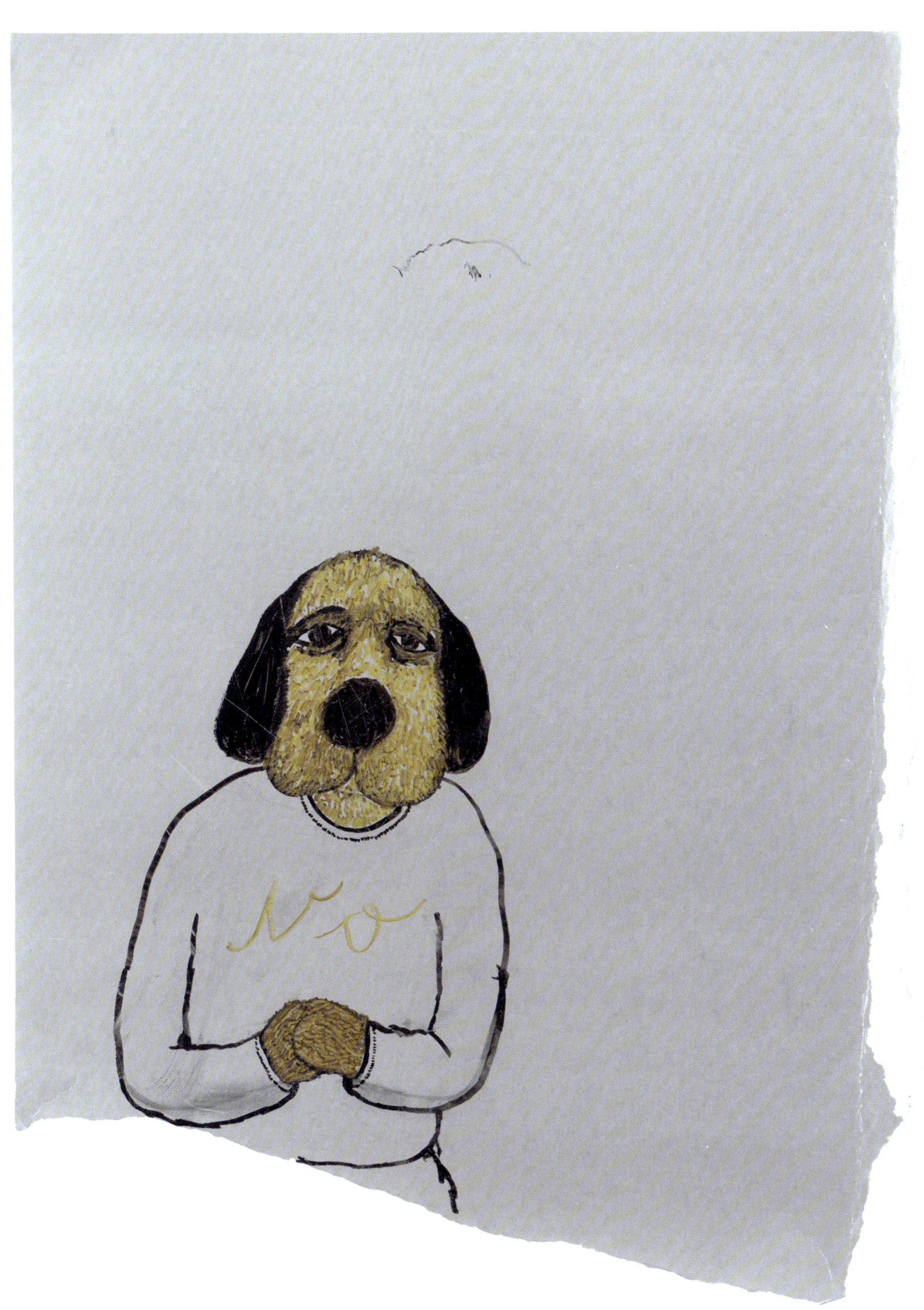
No

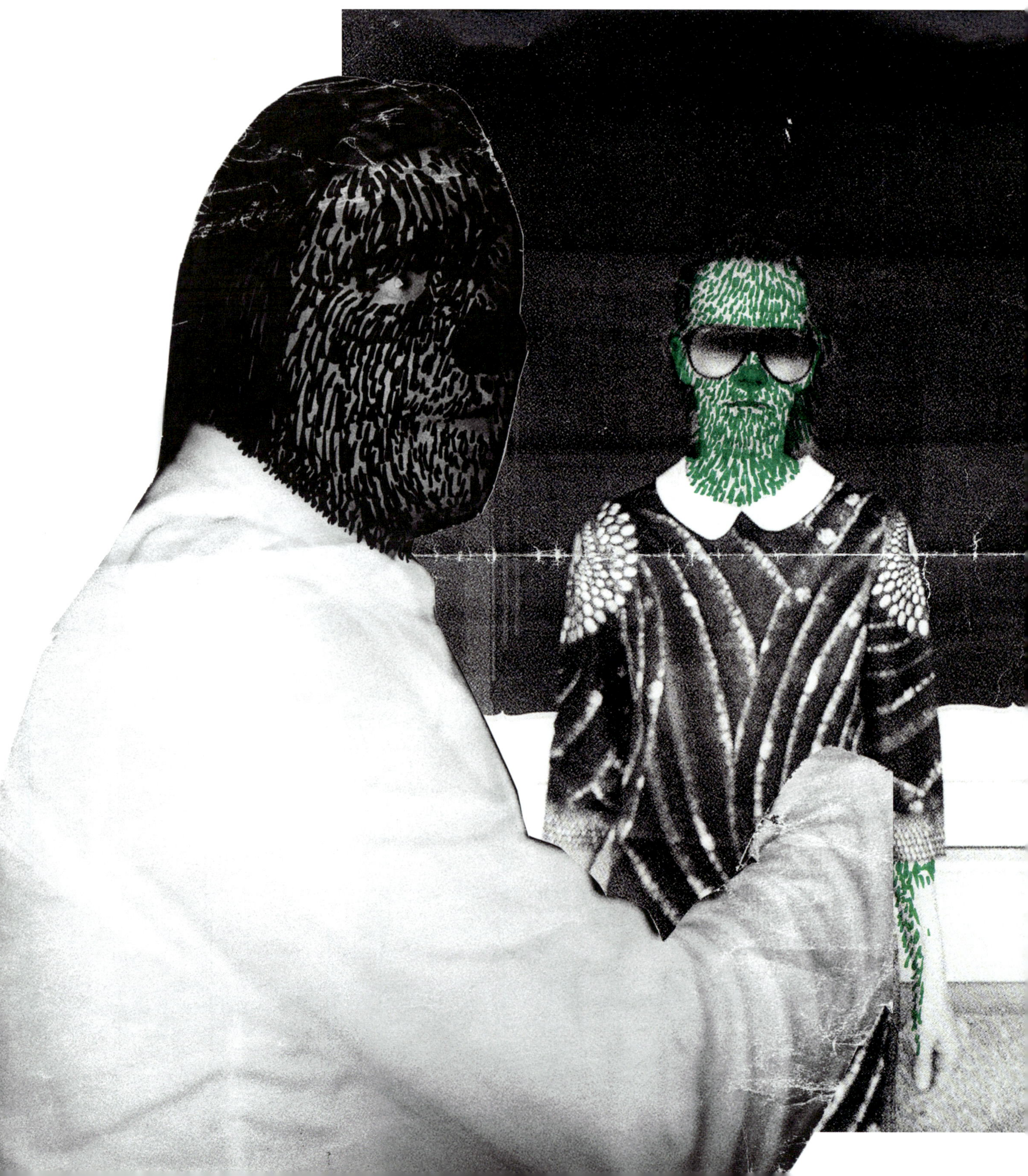

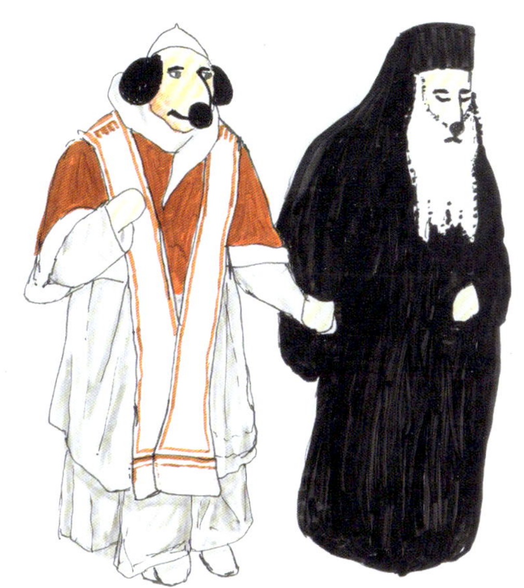

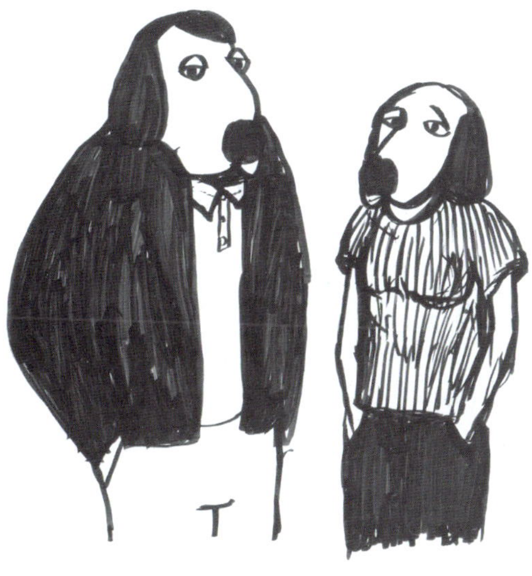

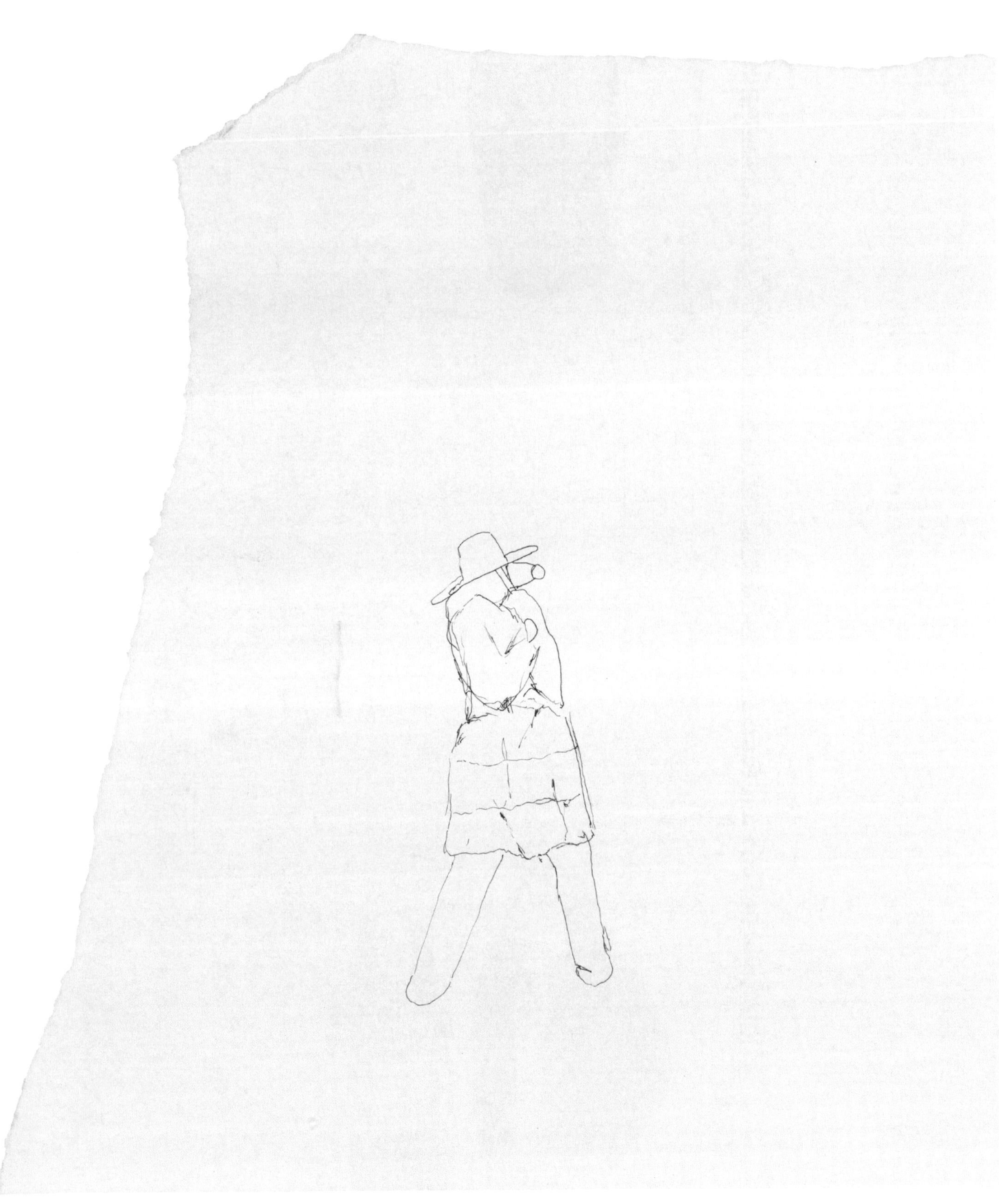

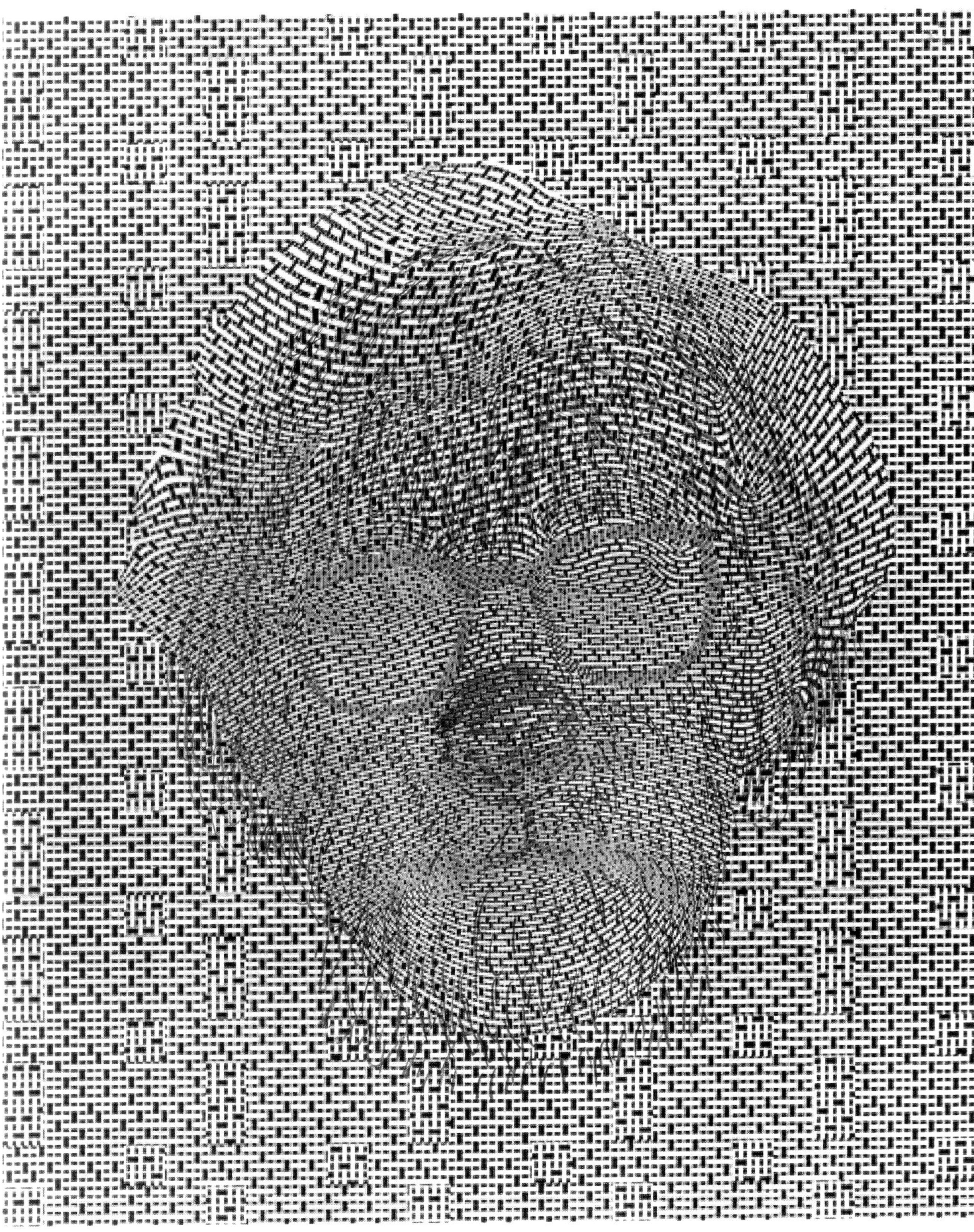

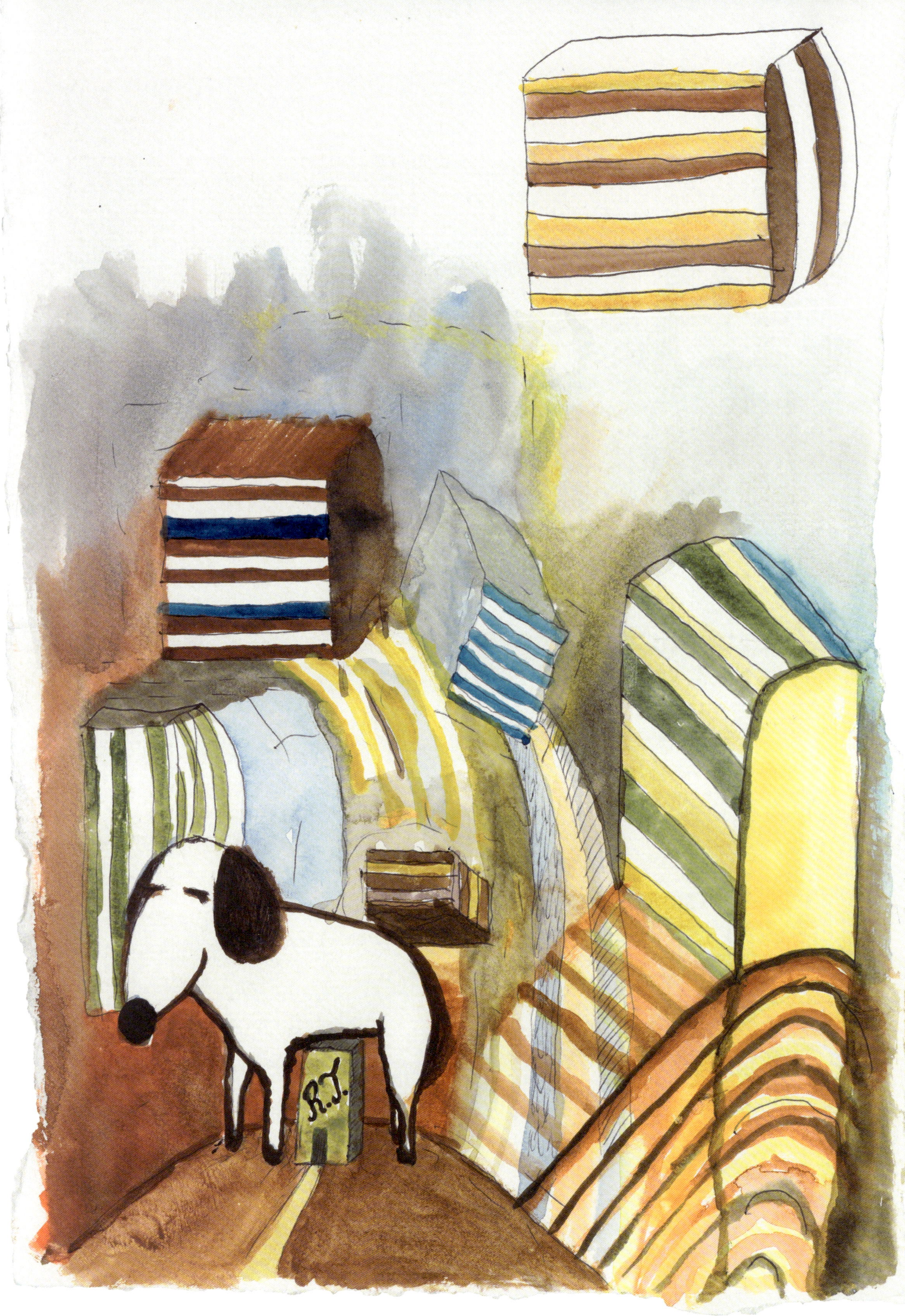

R.J.

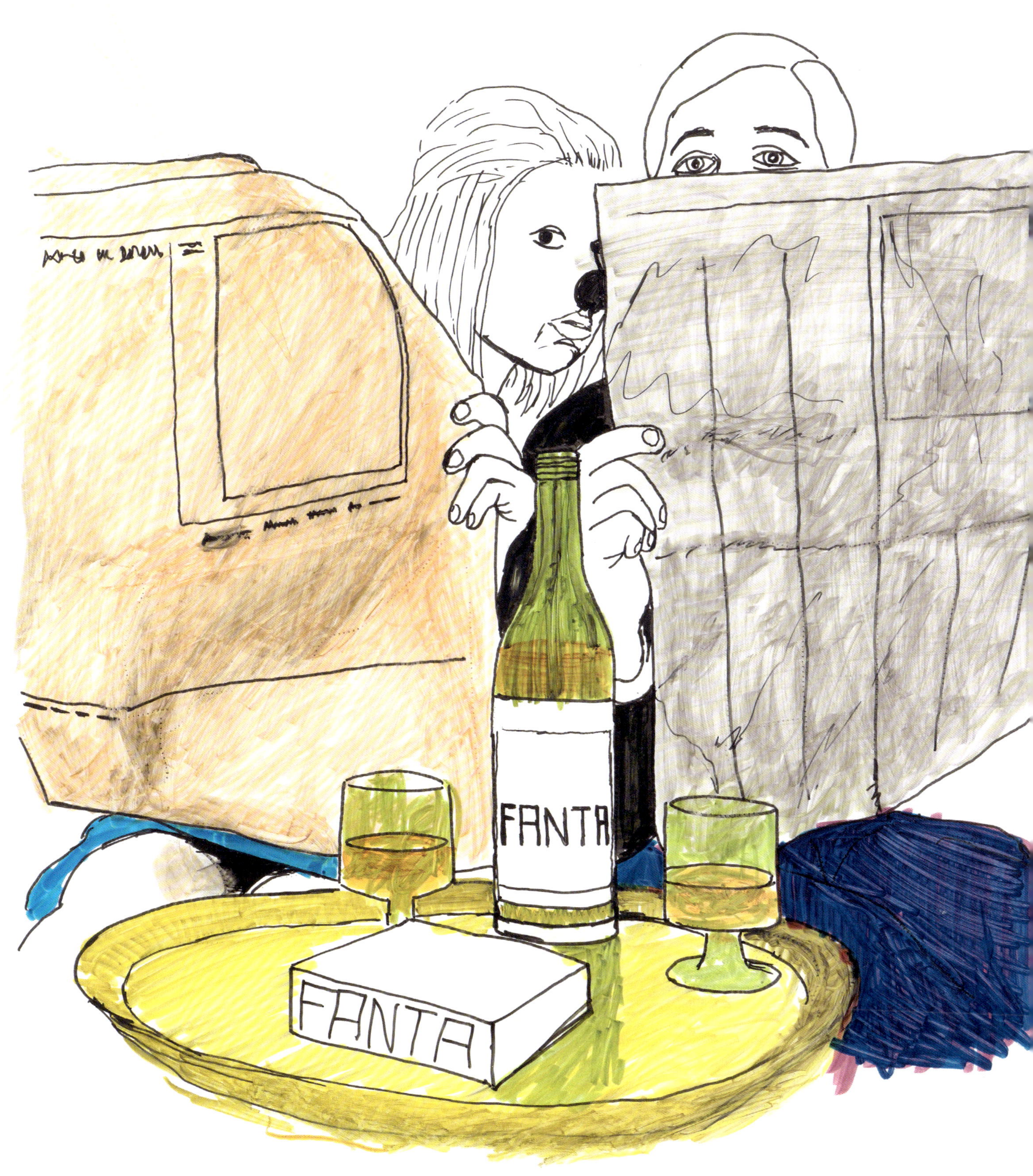
FANTA
FANTA

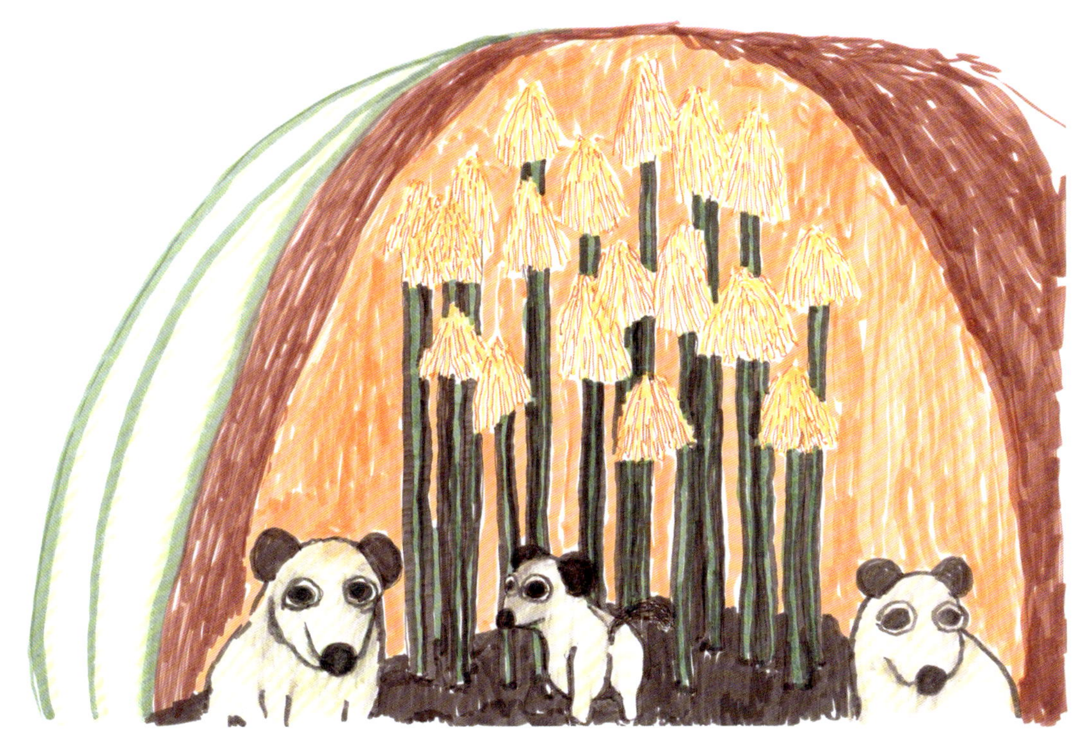

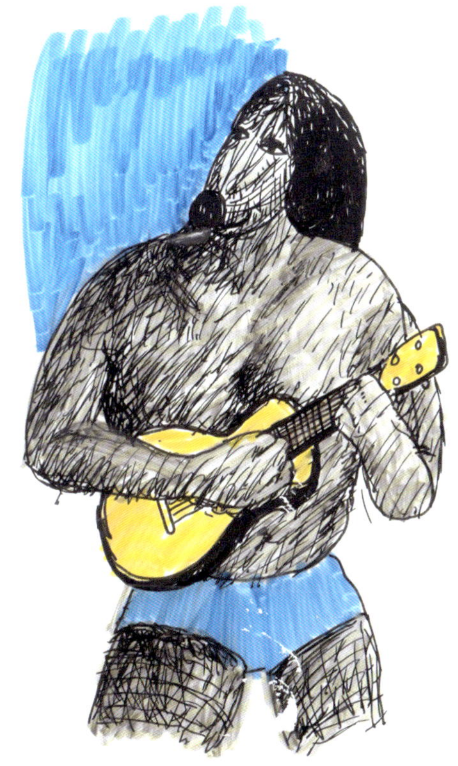

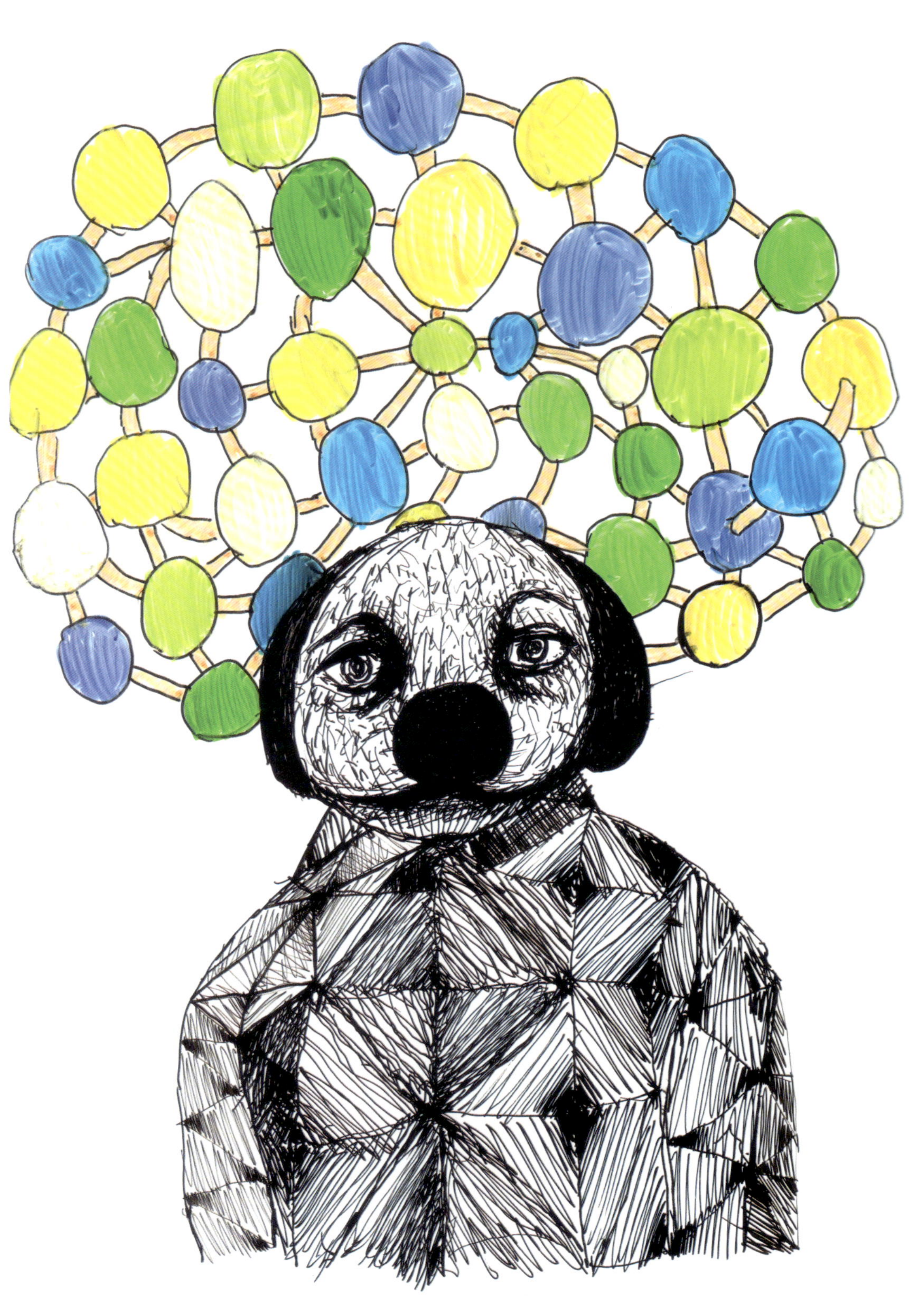

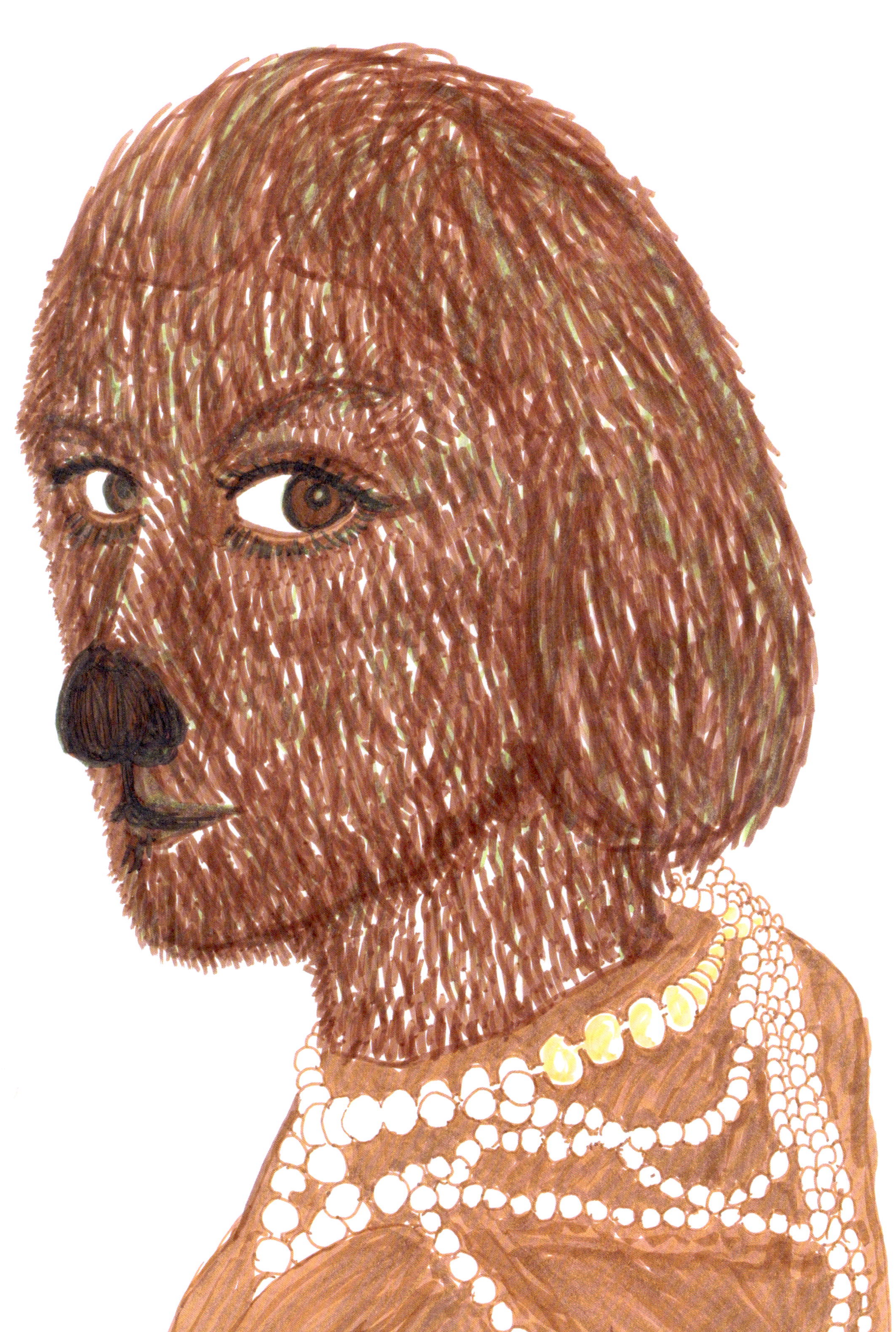

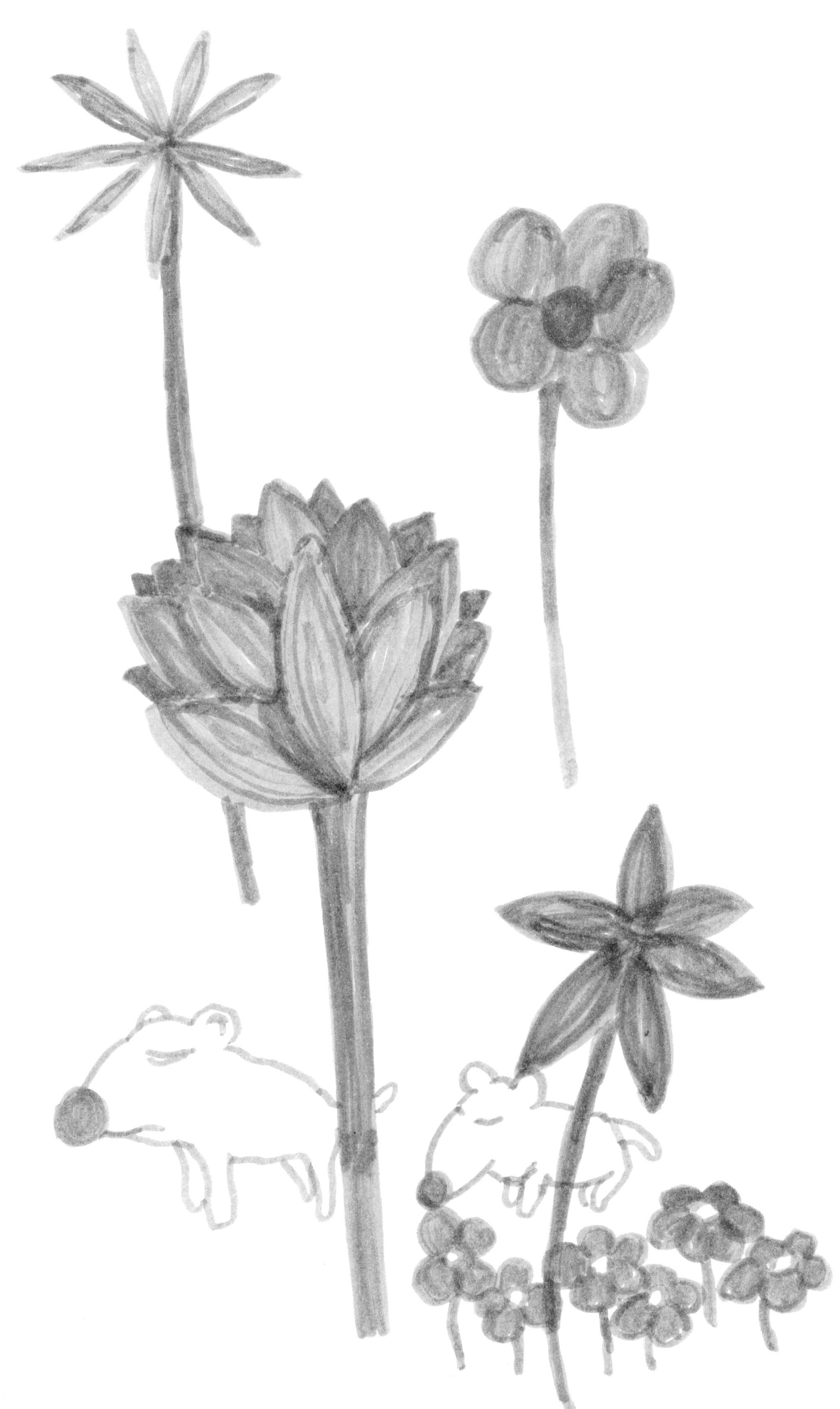

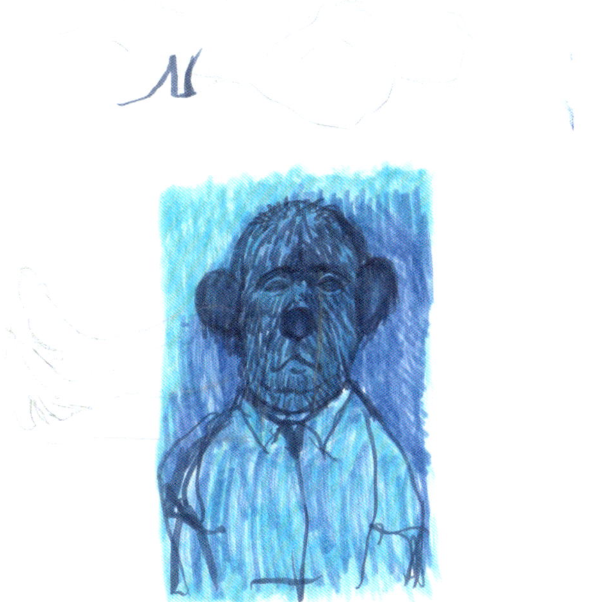

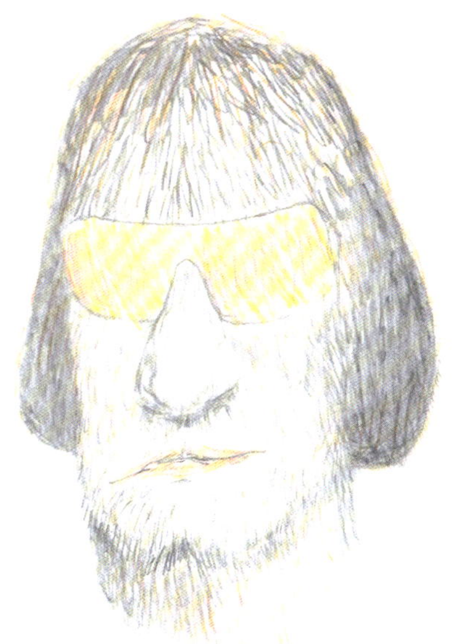

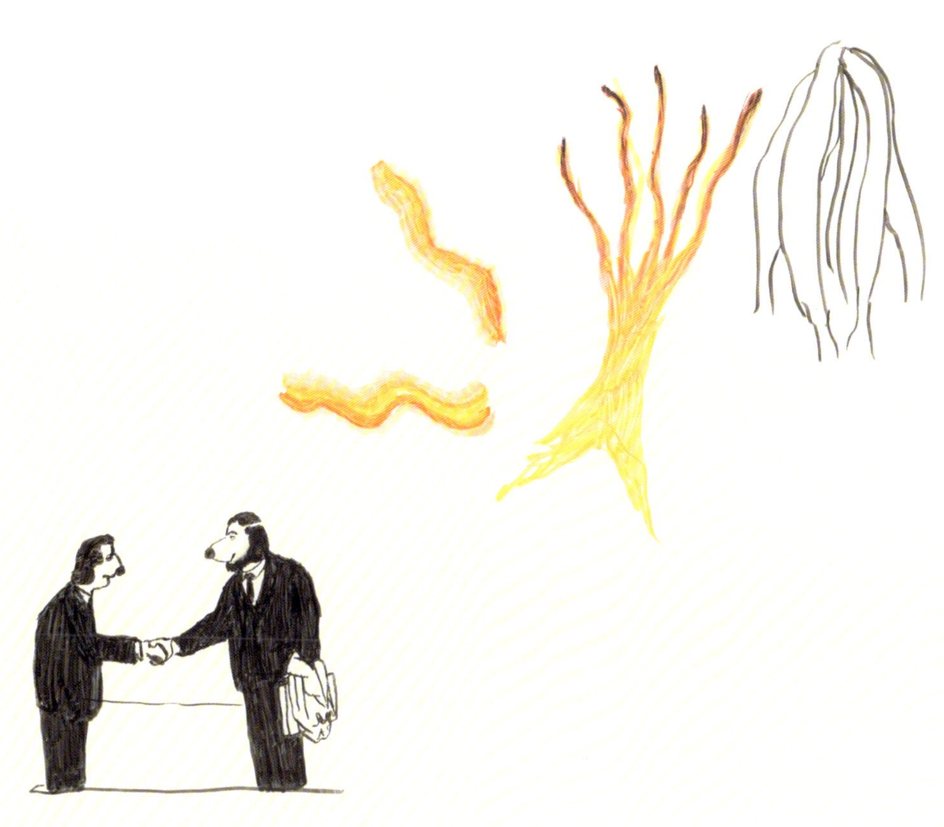

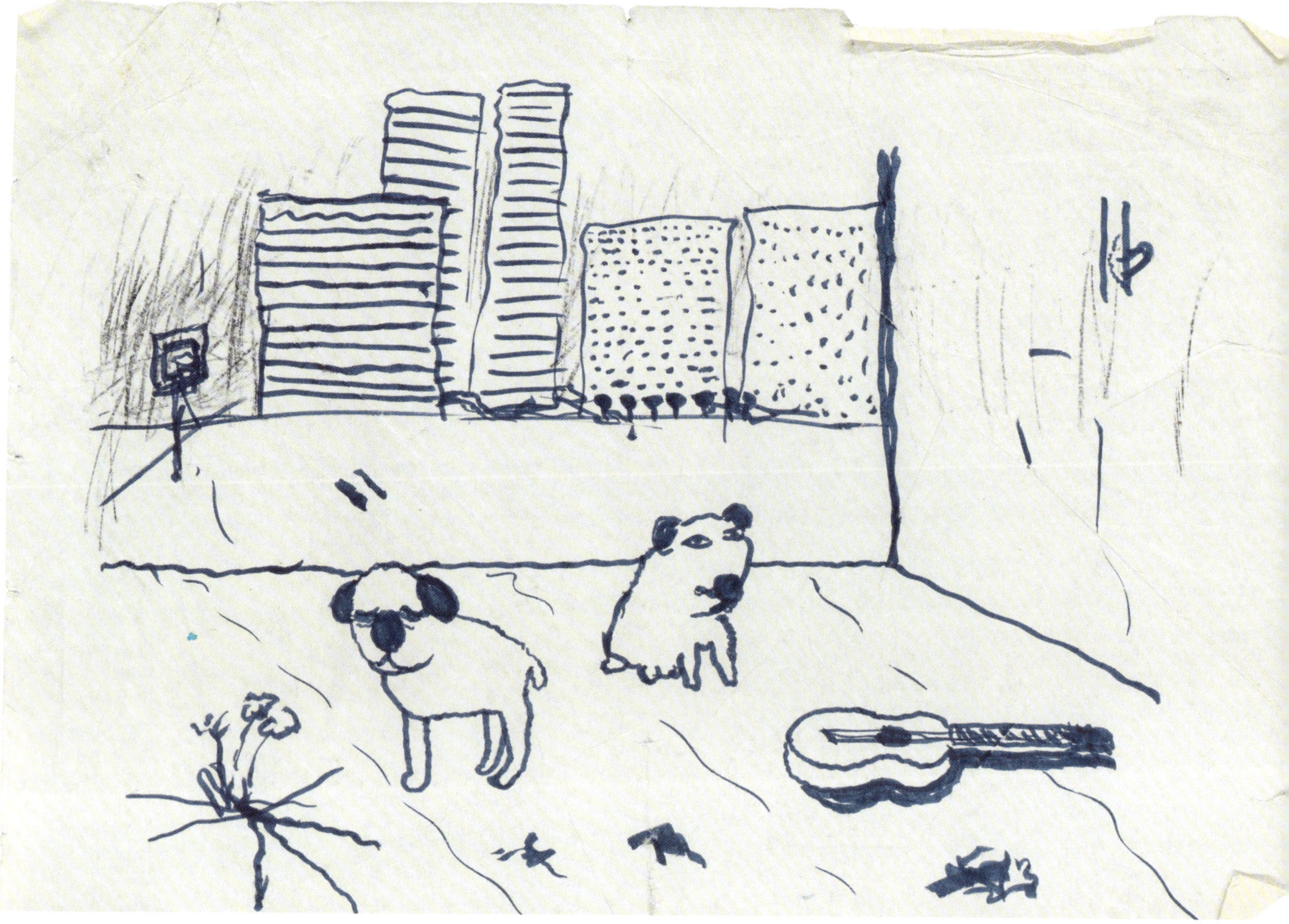

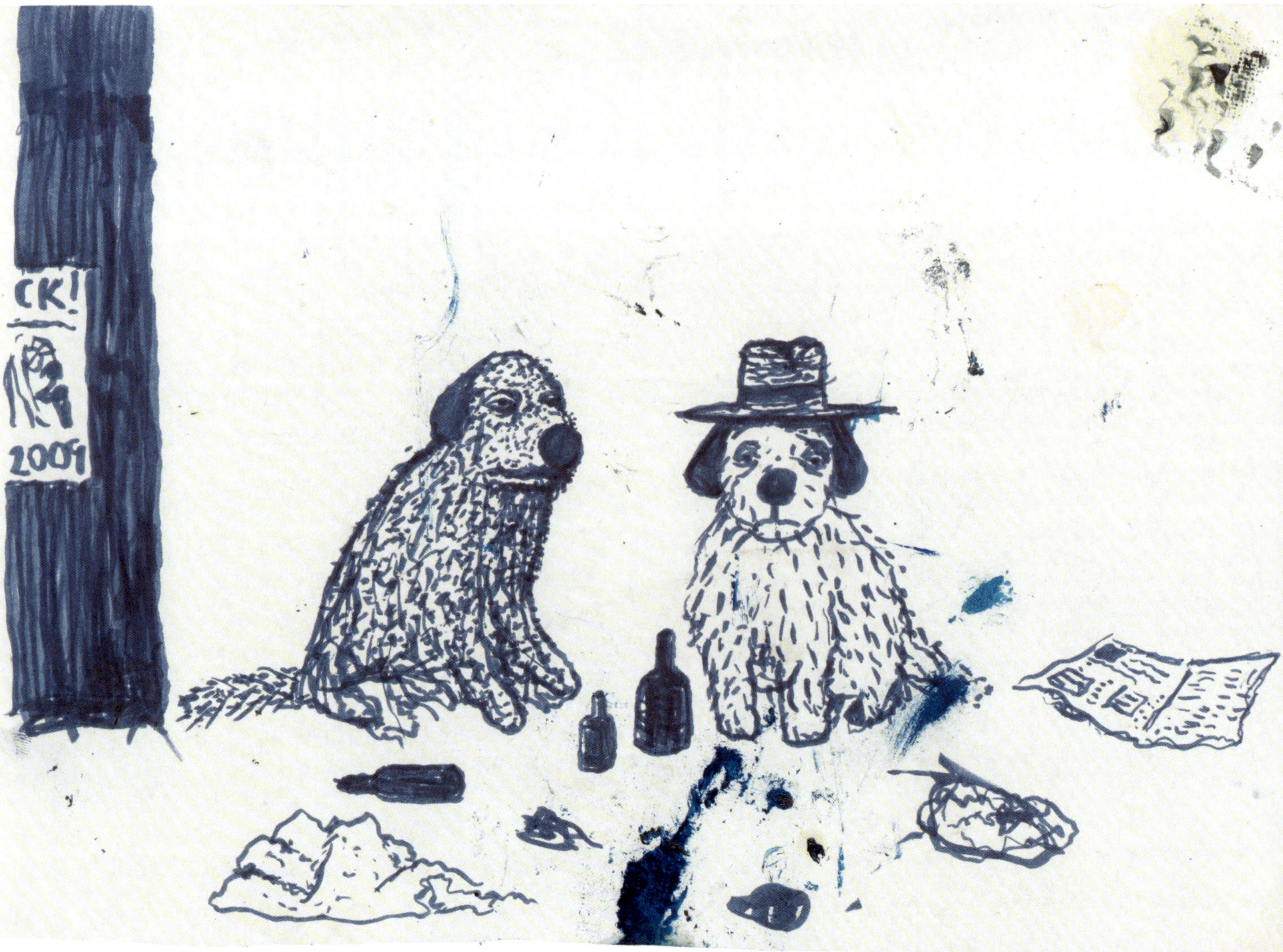

CK!
2001

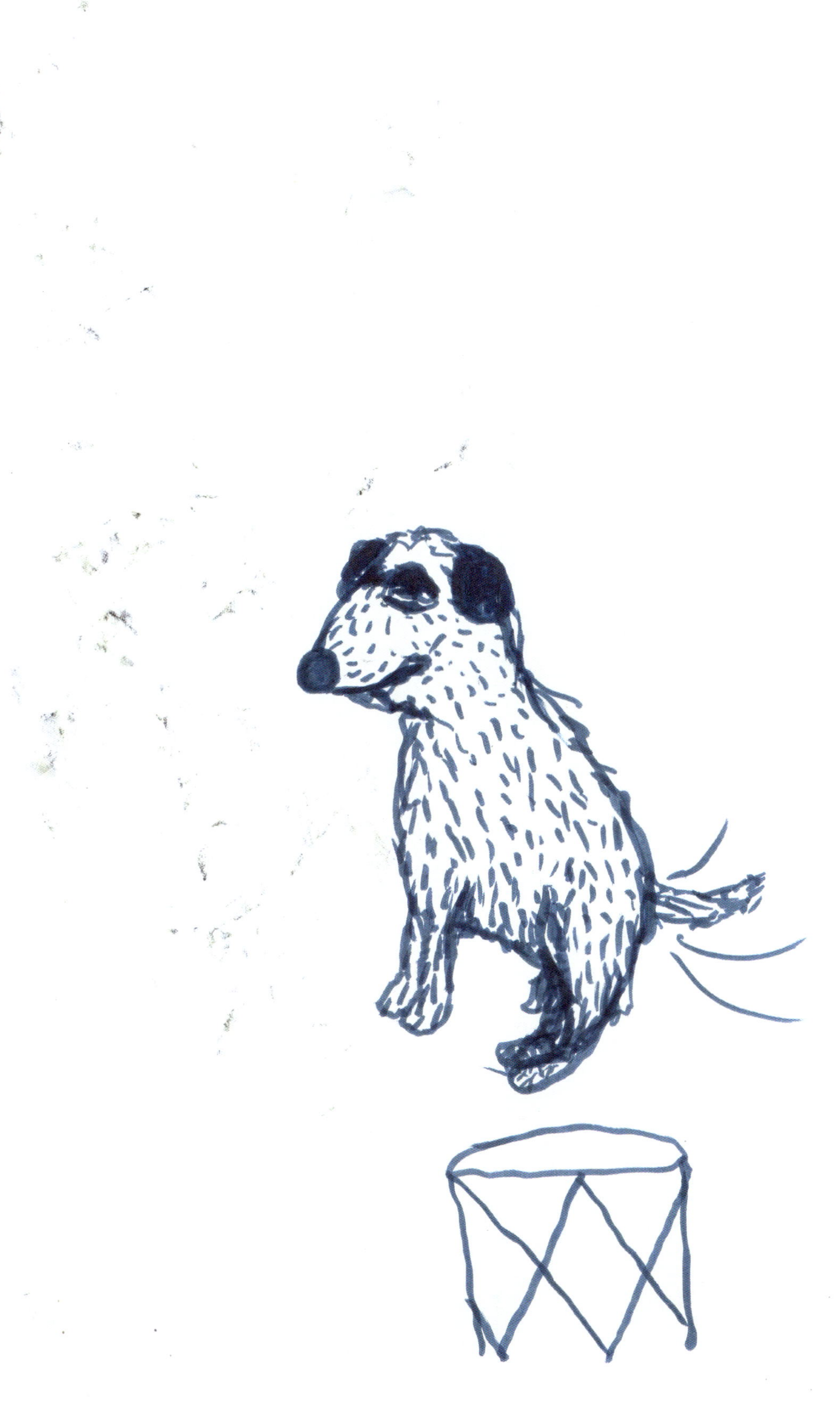

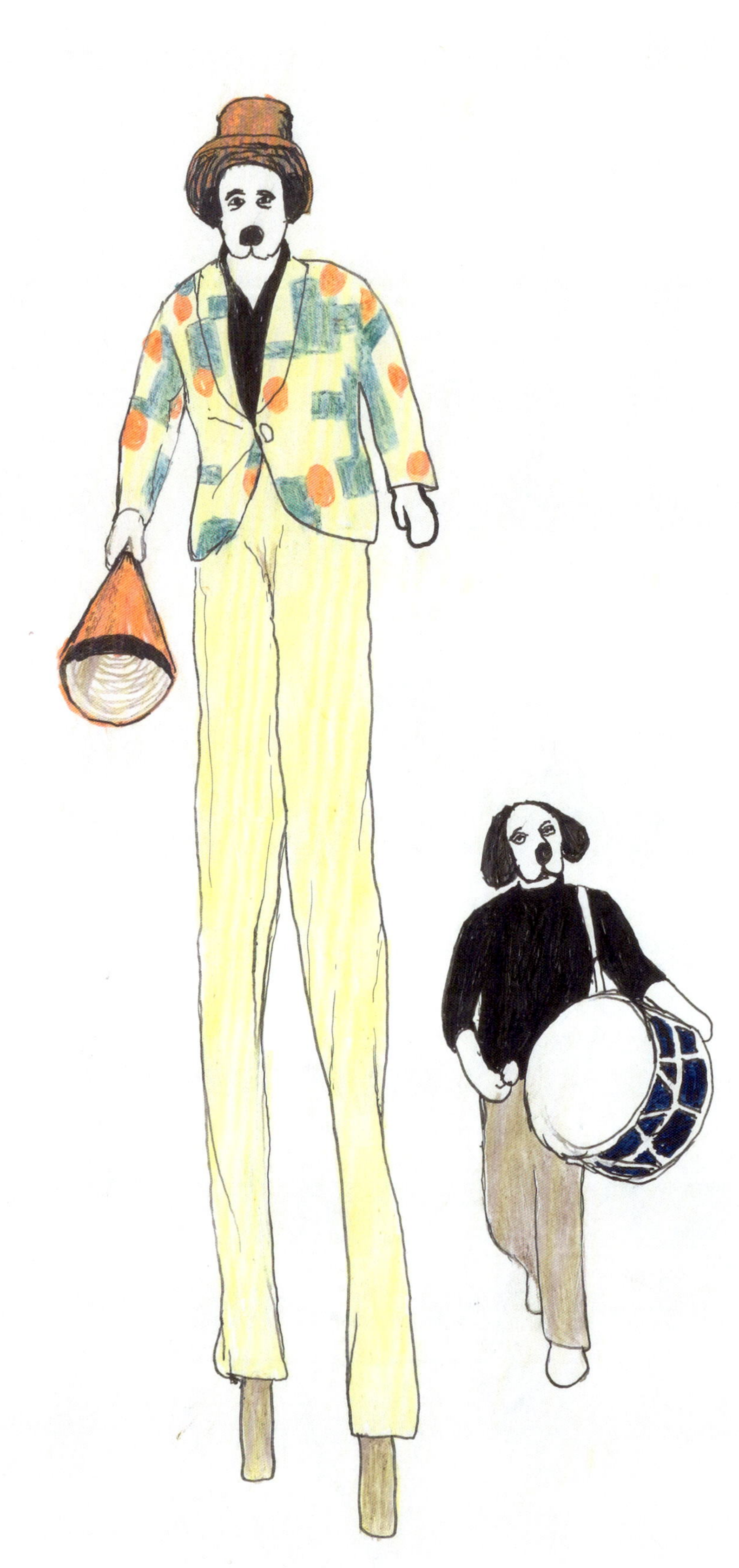

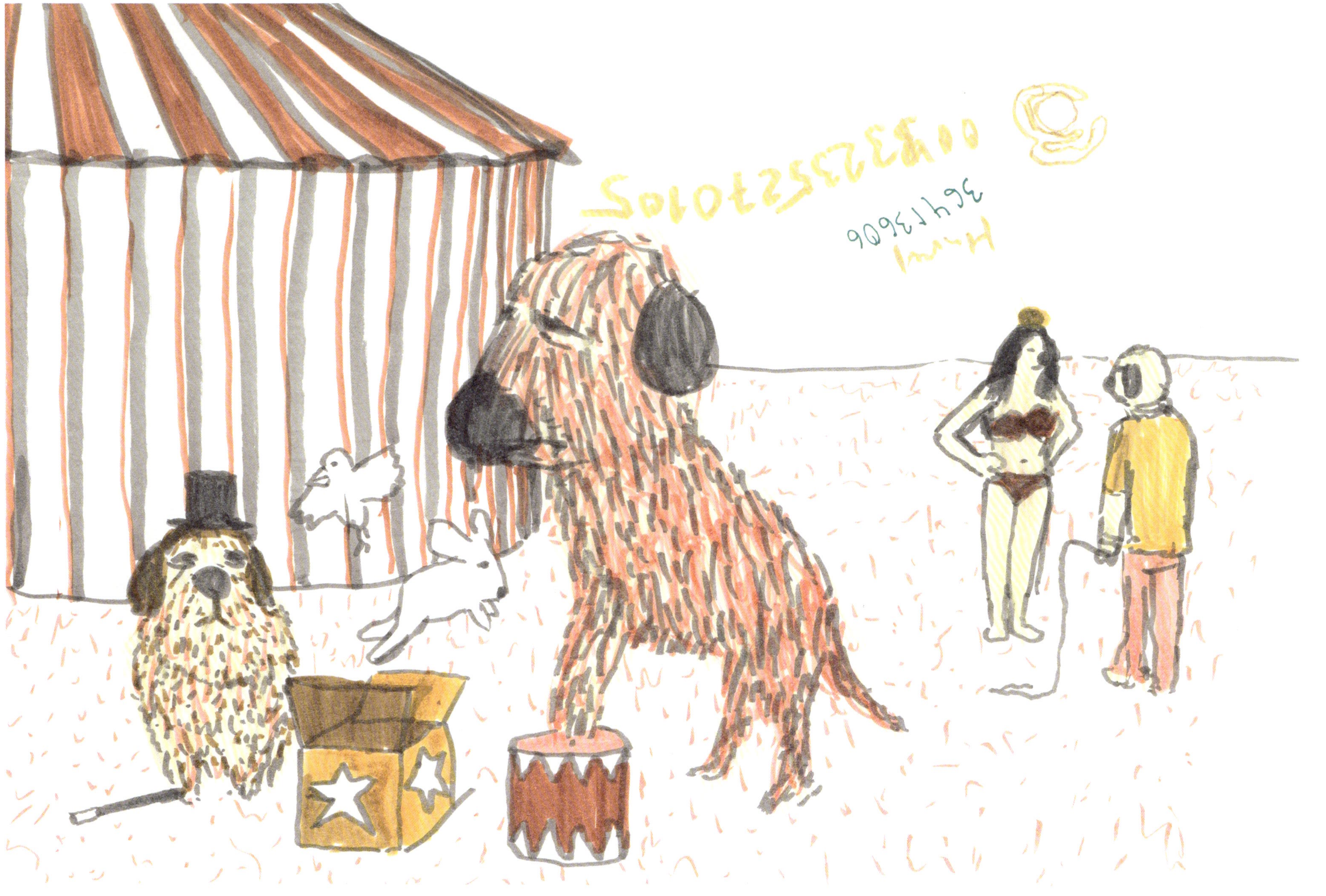
Hanni
36413606
0093235270105

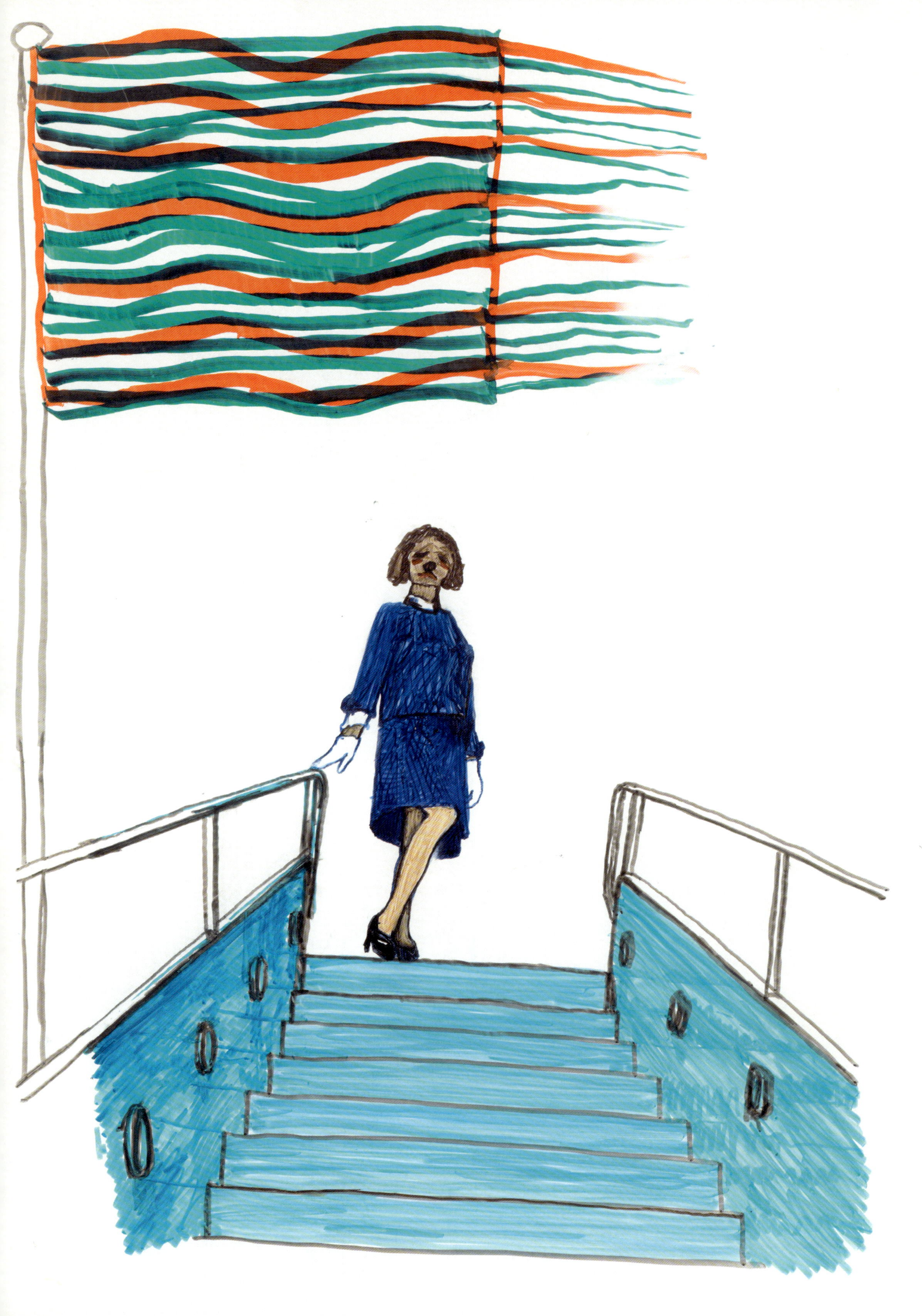

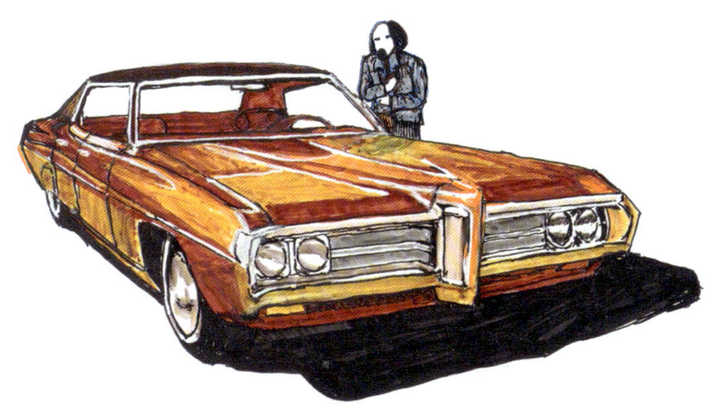
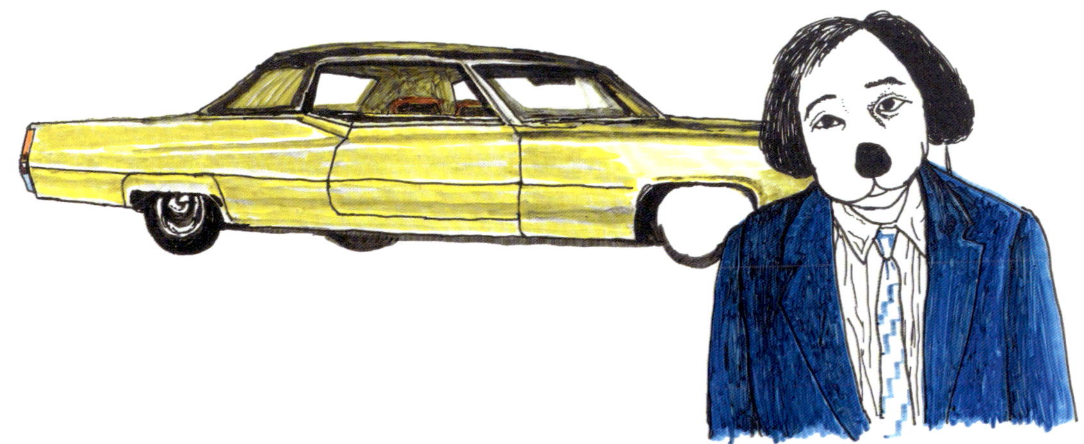

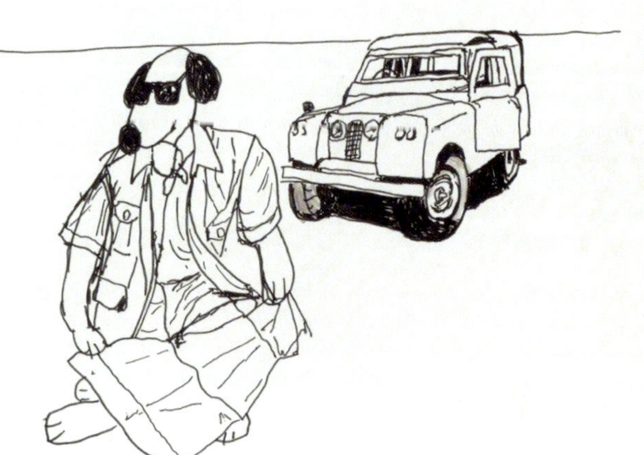

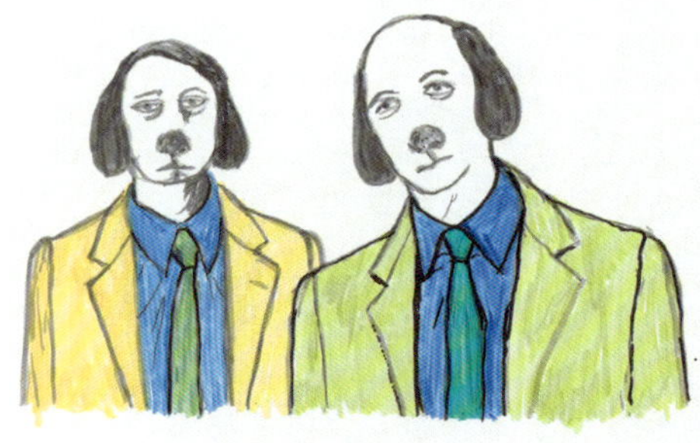

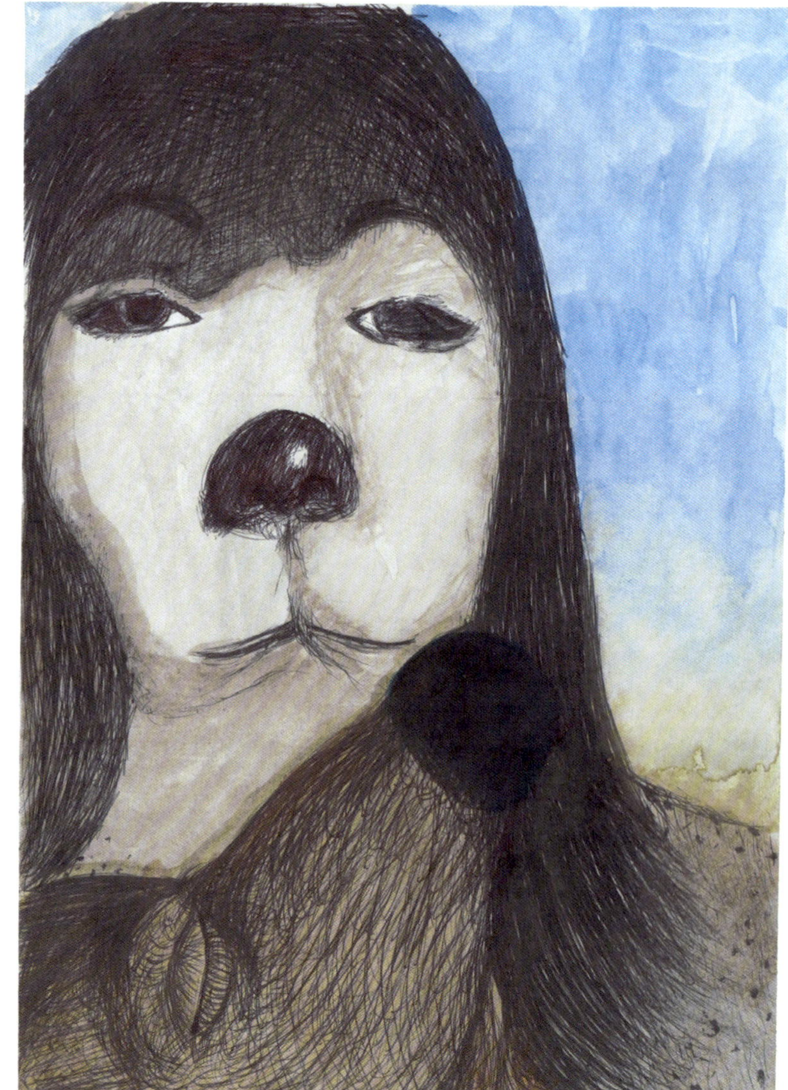

Dogs noir
csl orange
Miami

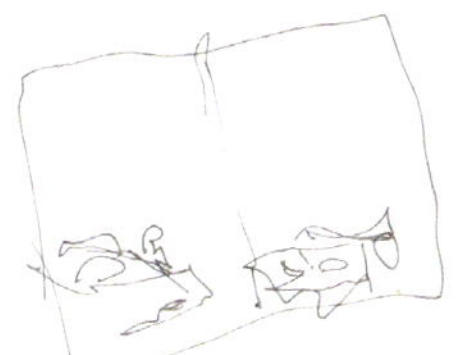

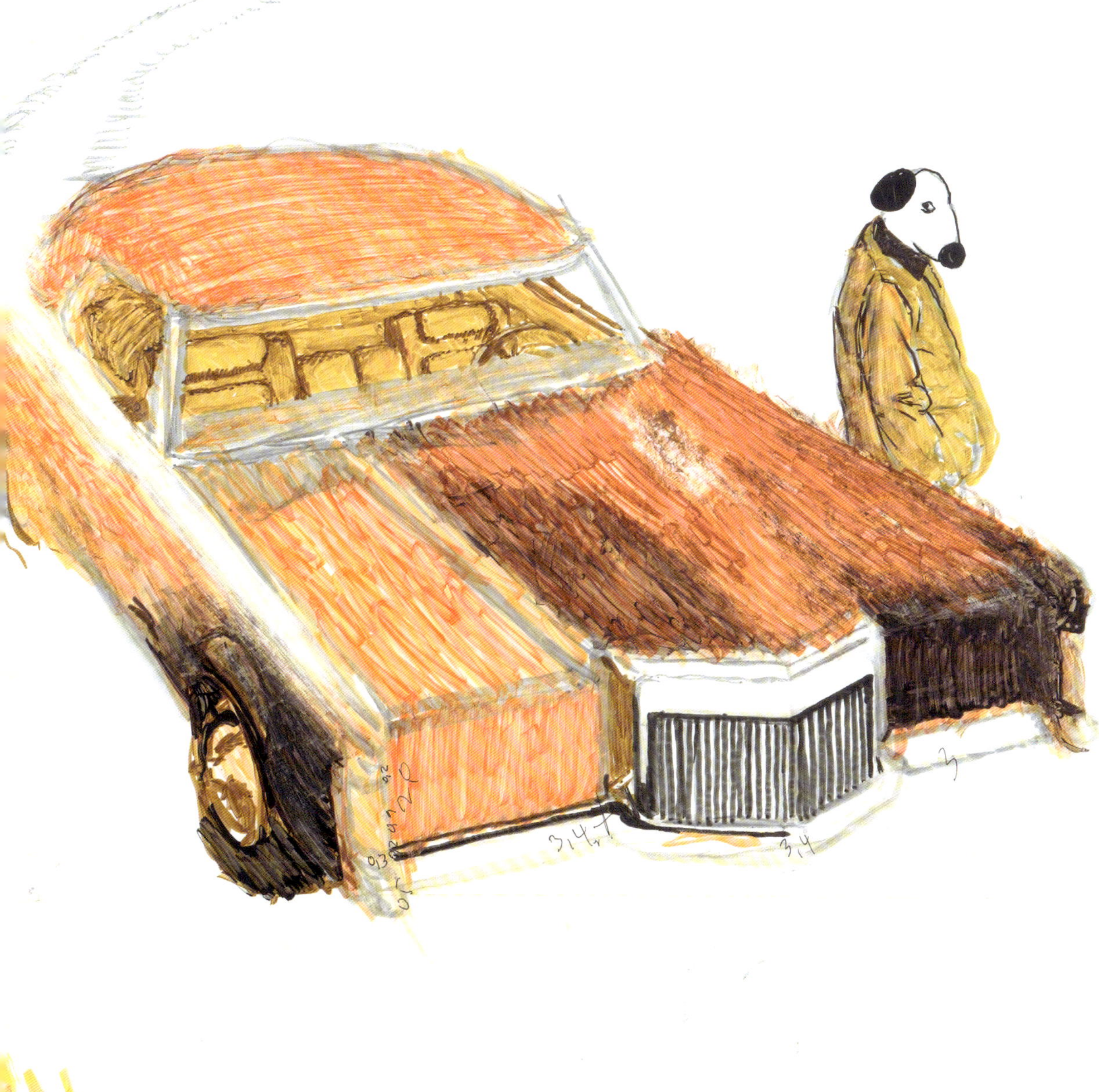

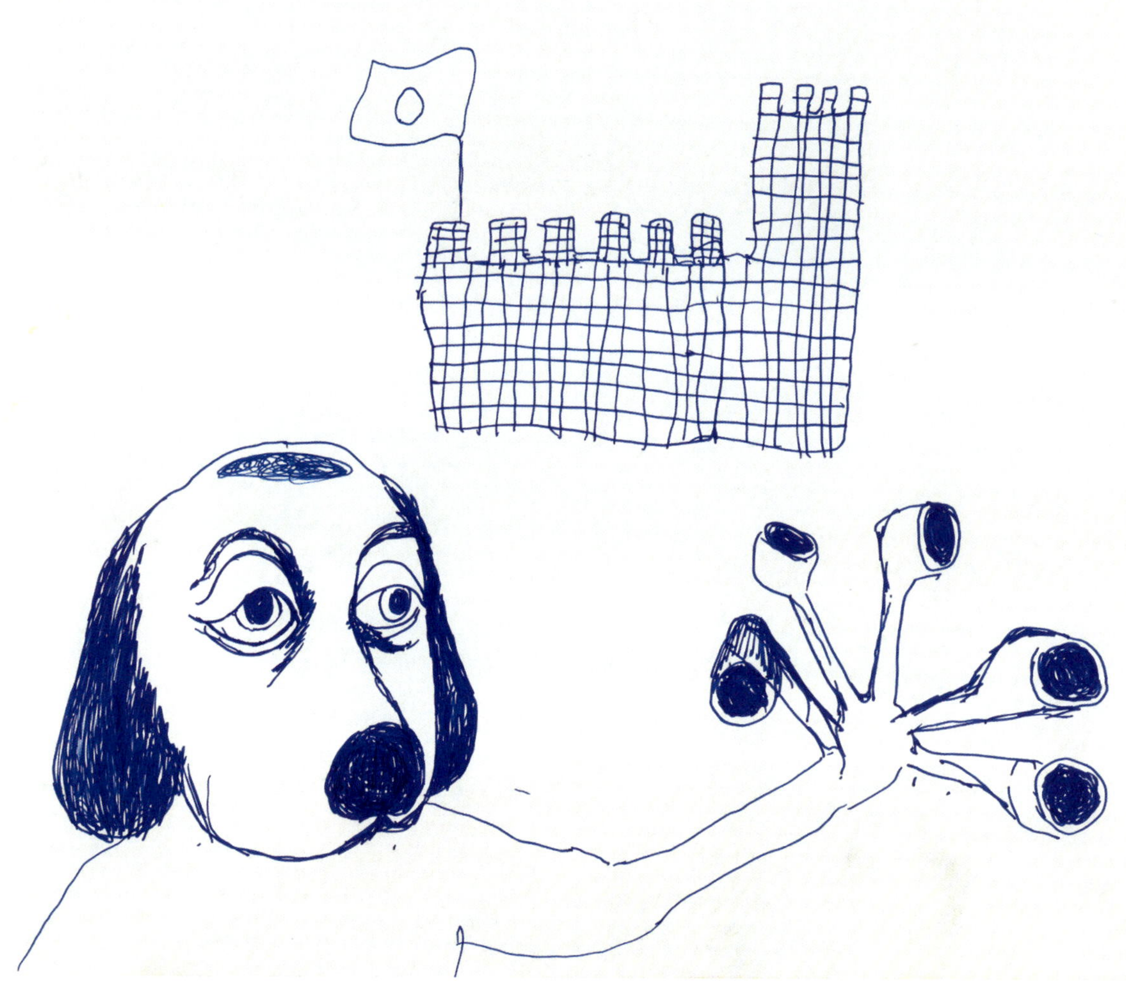

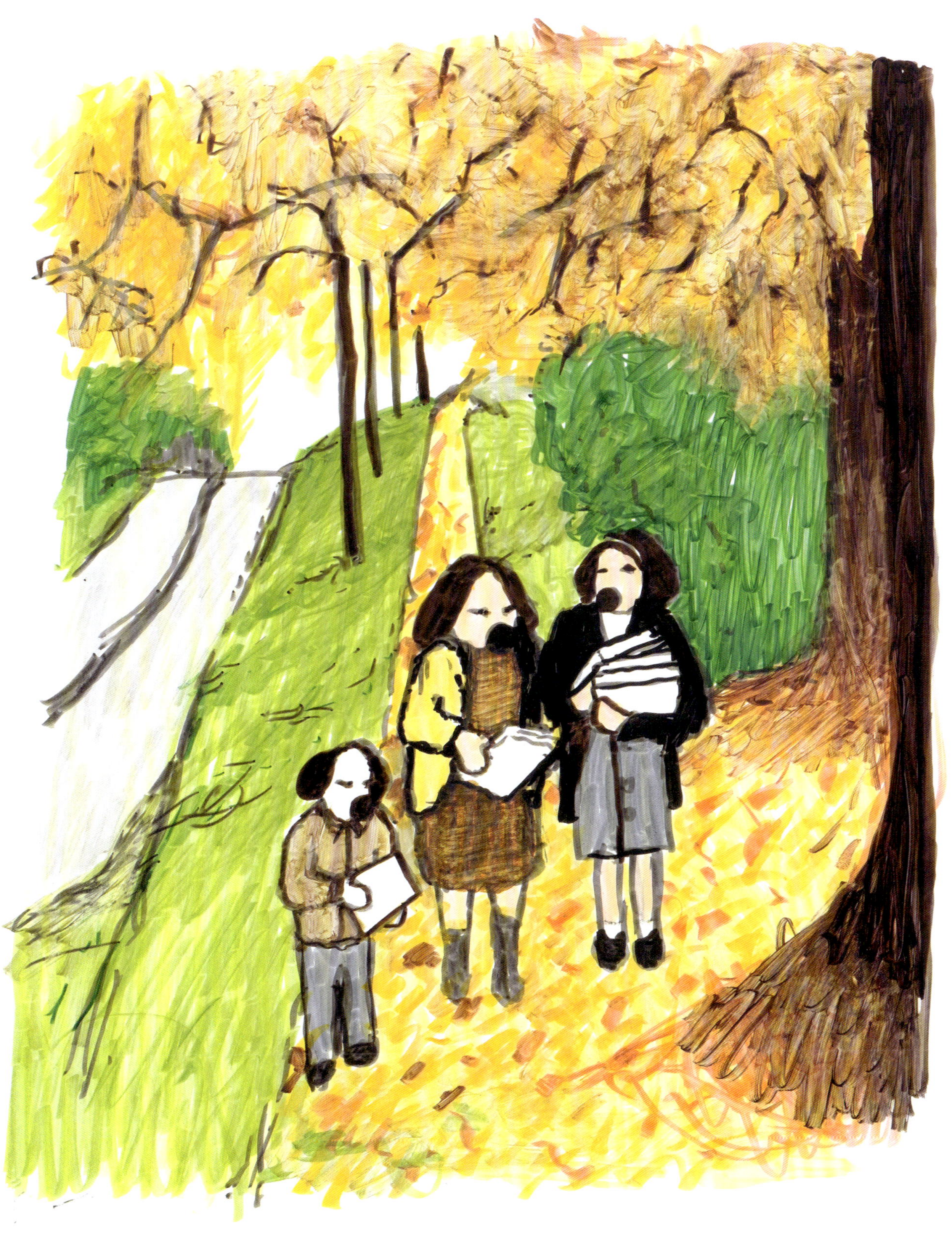

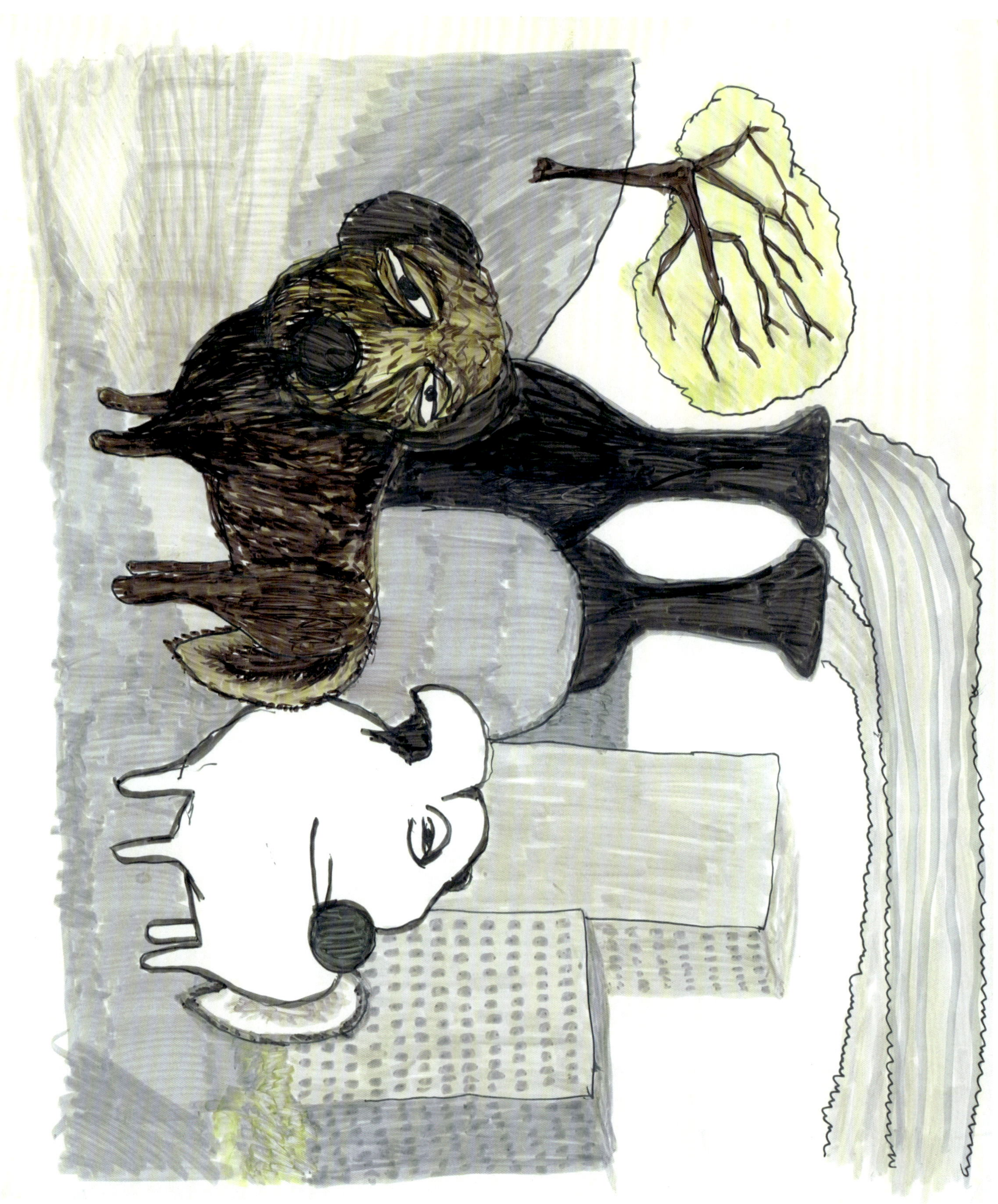

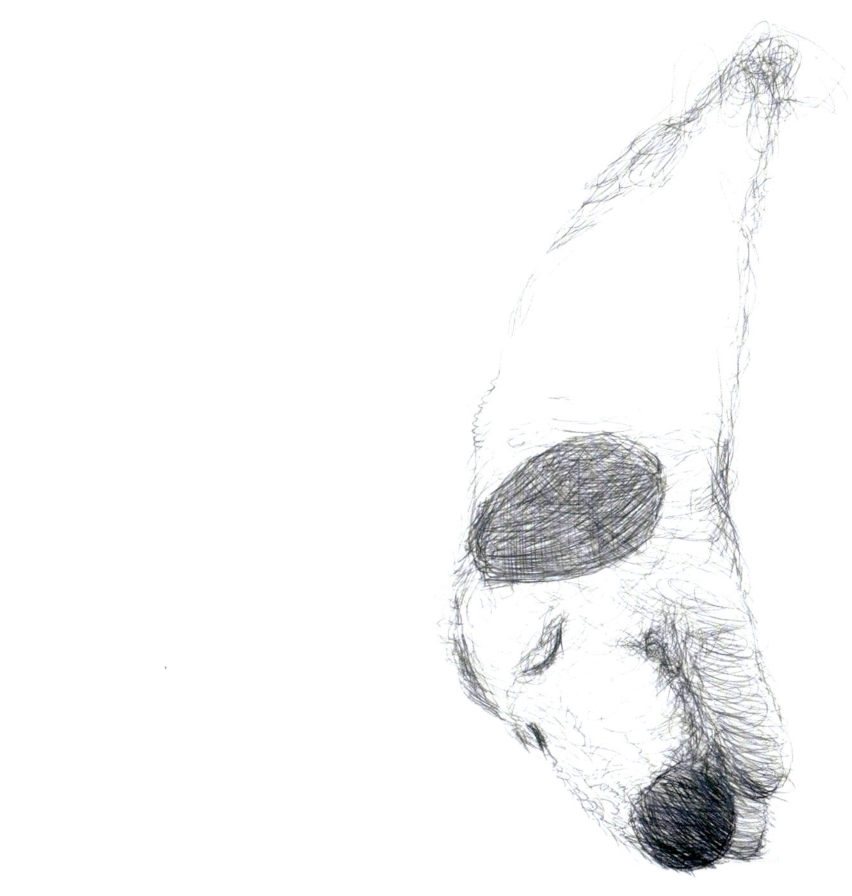

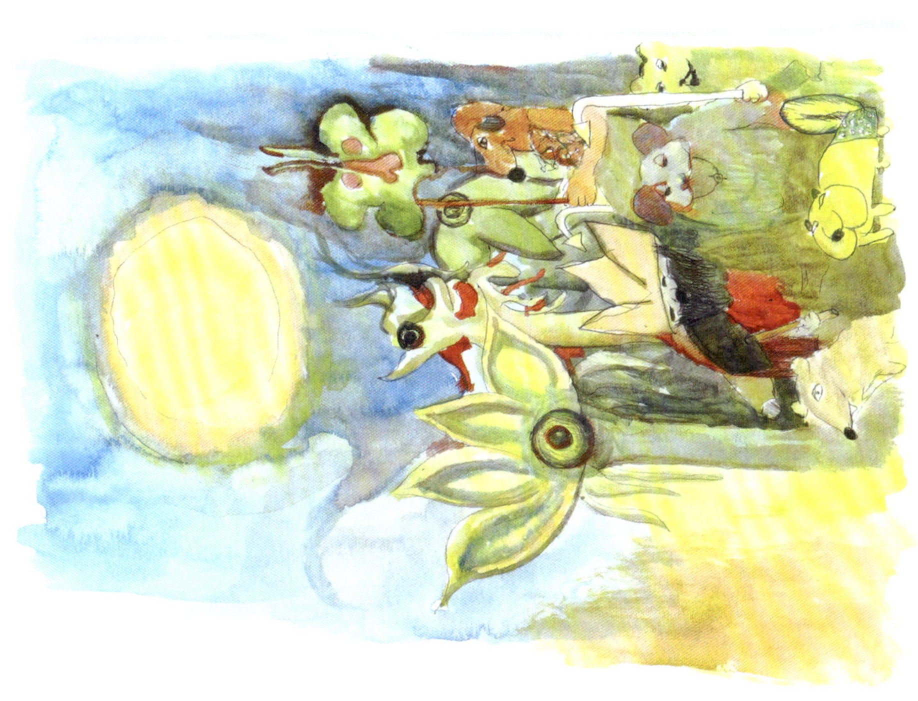

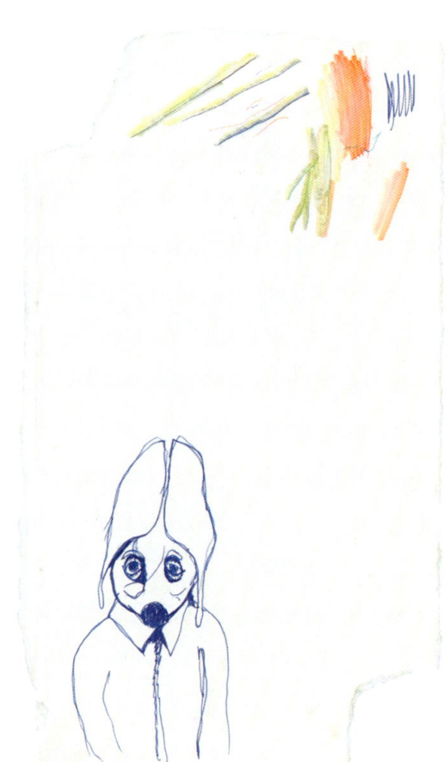

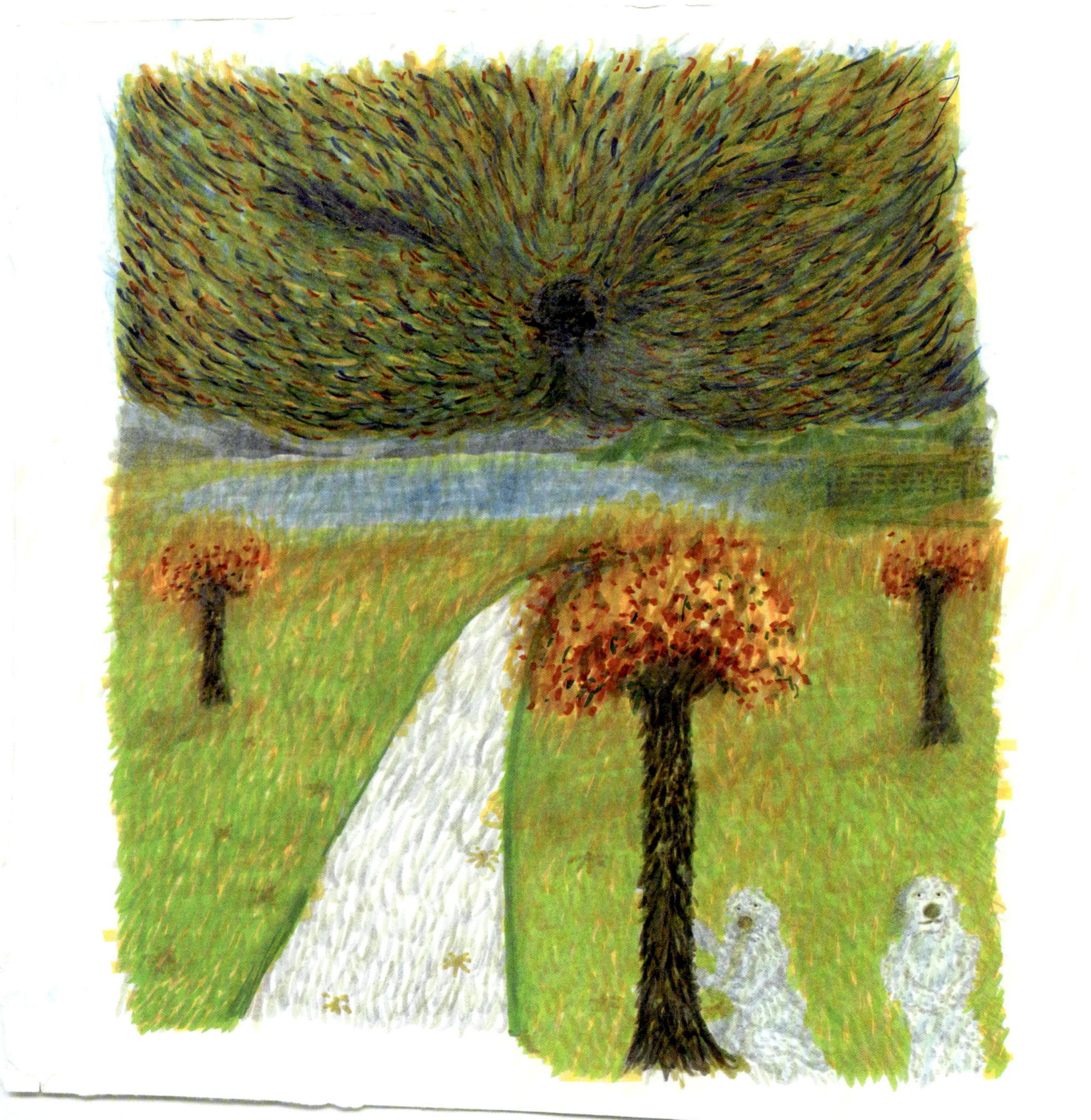

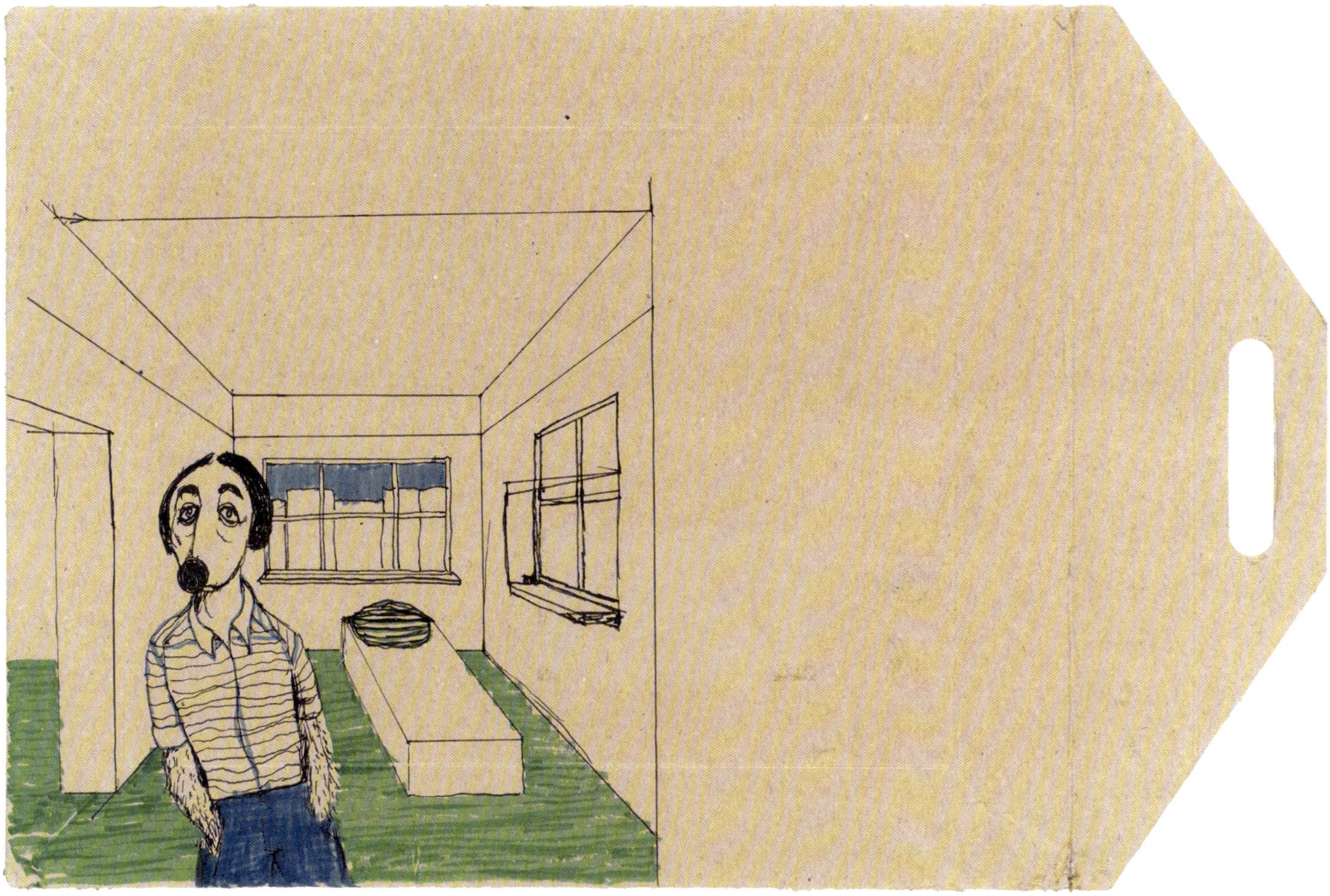

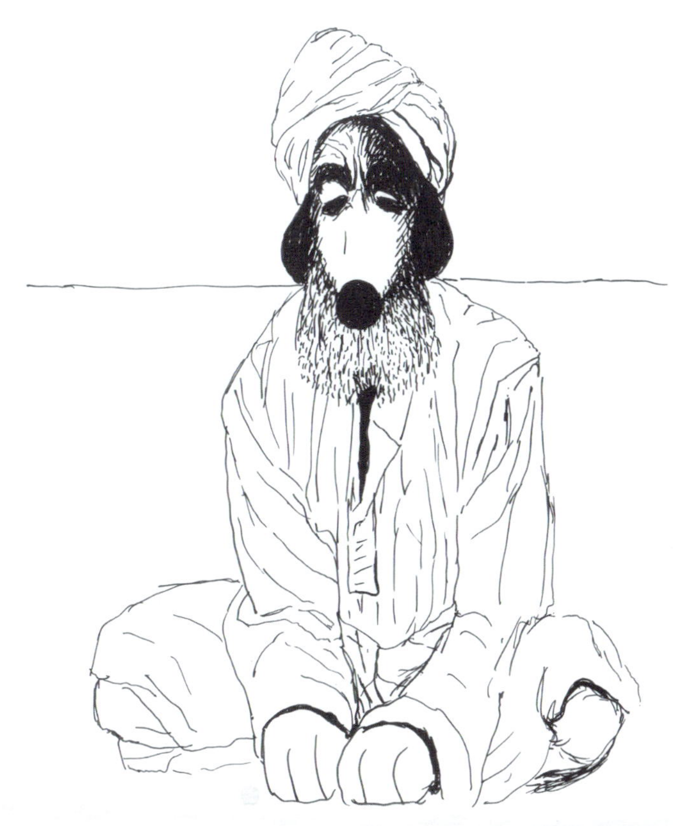

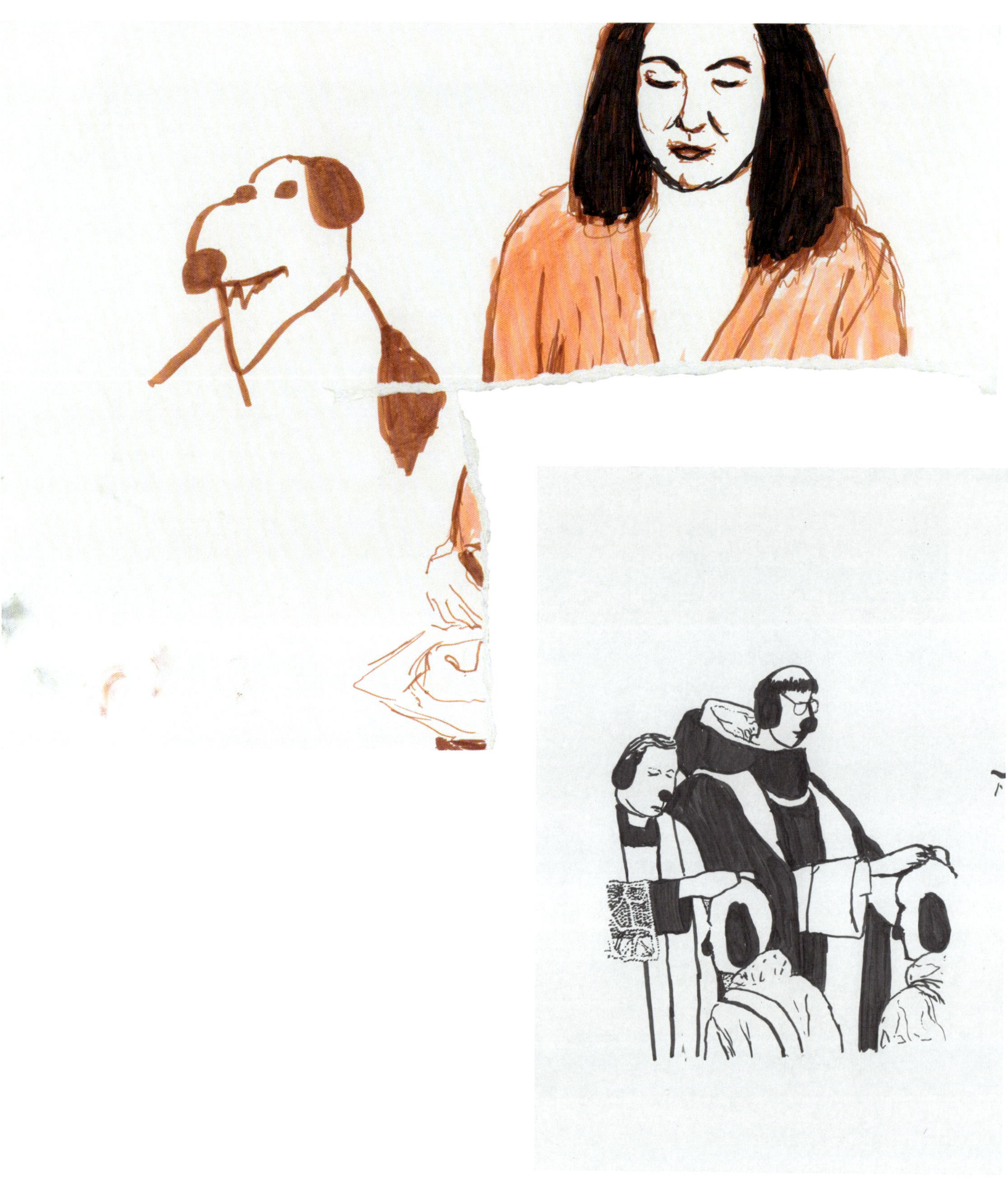

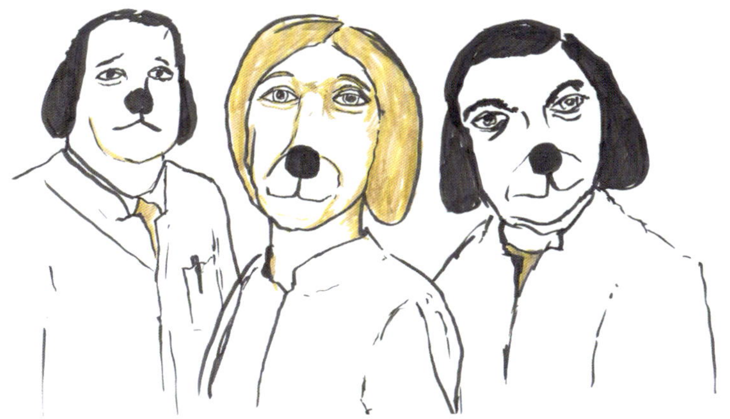

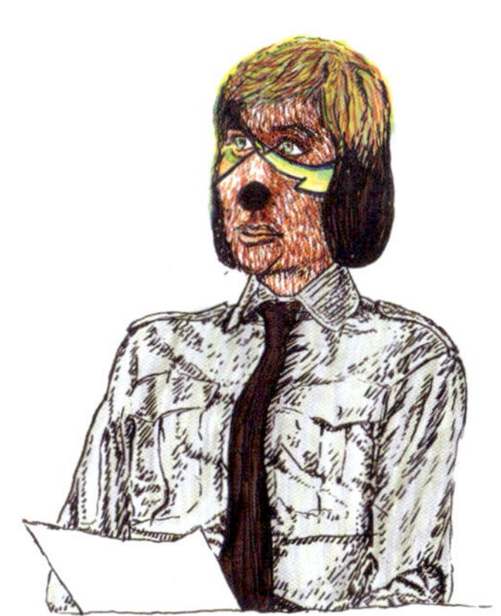

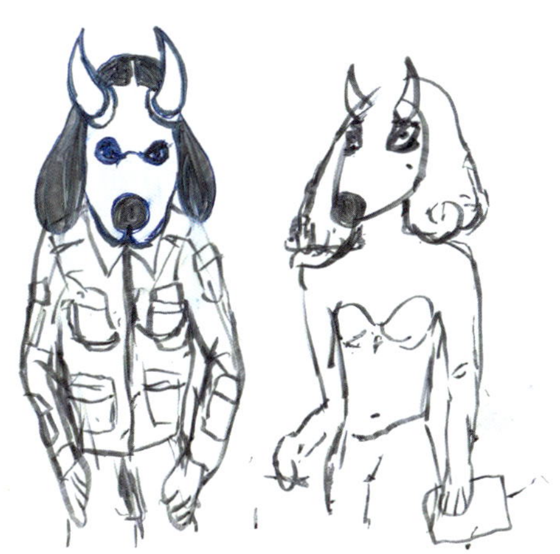

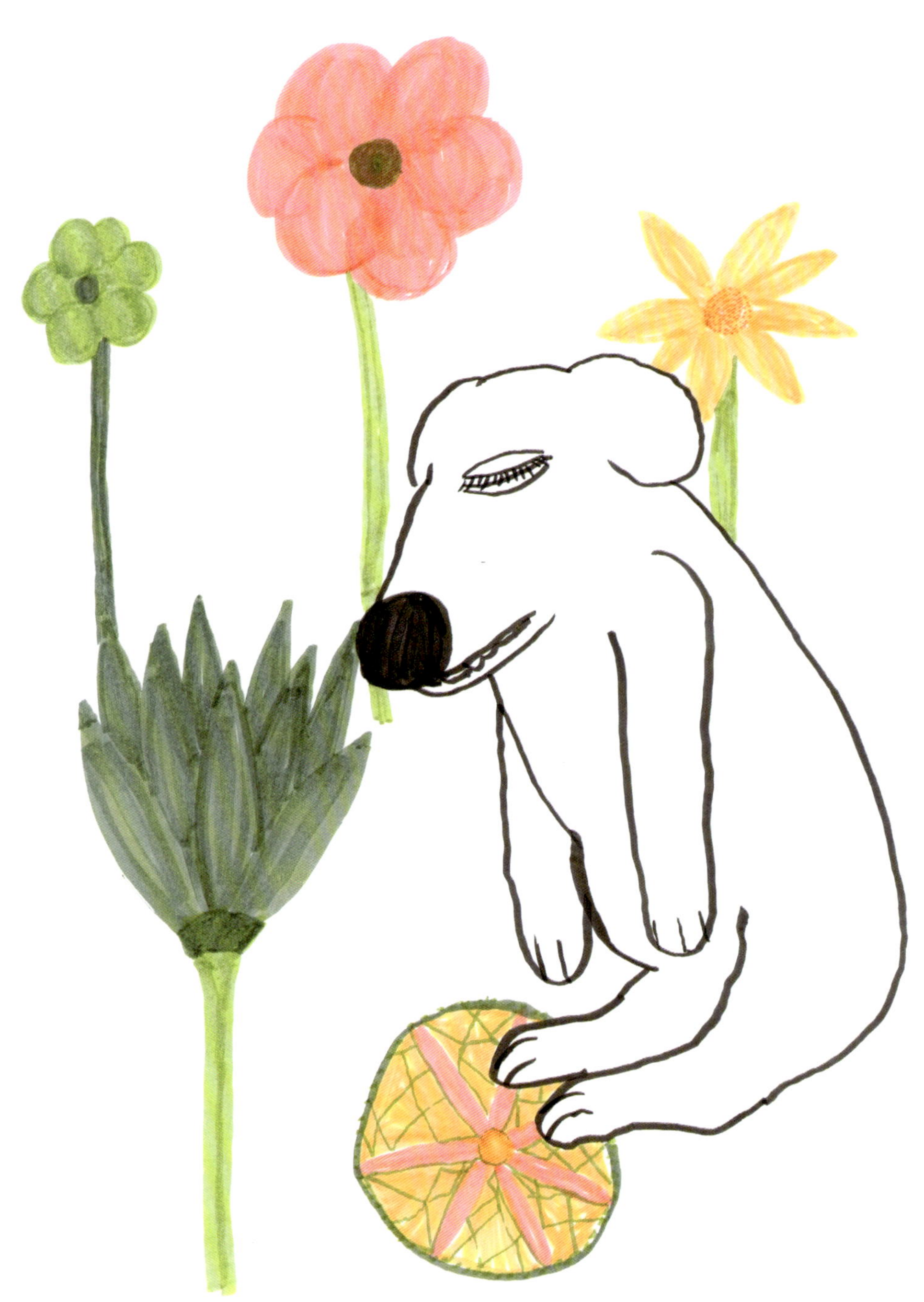

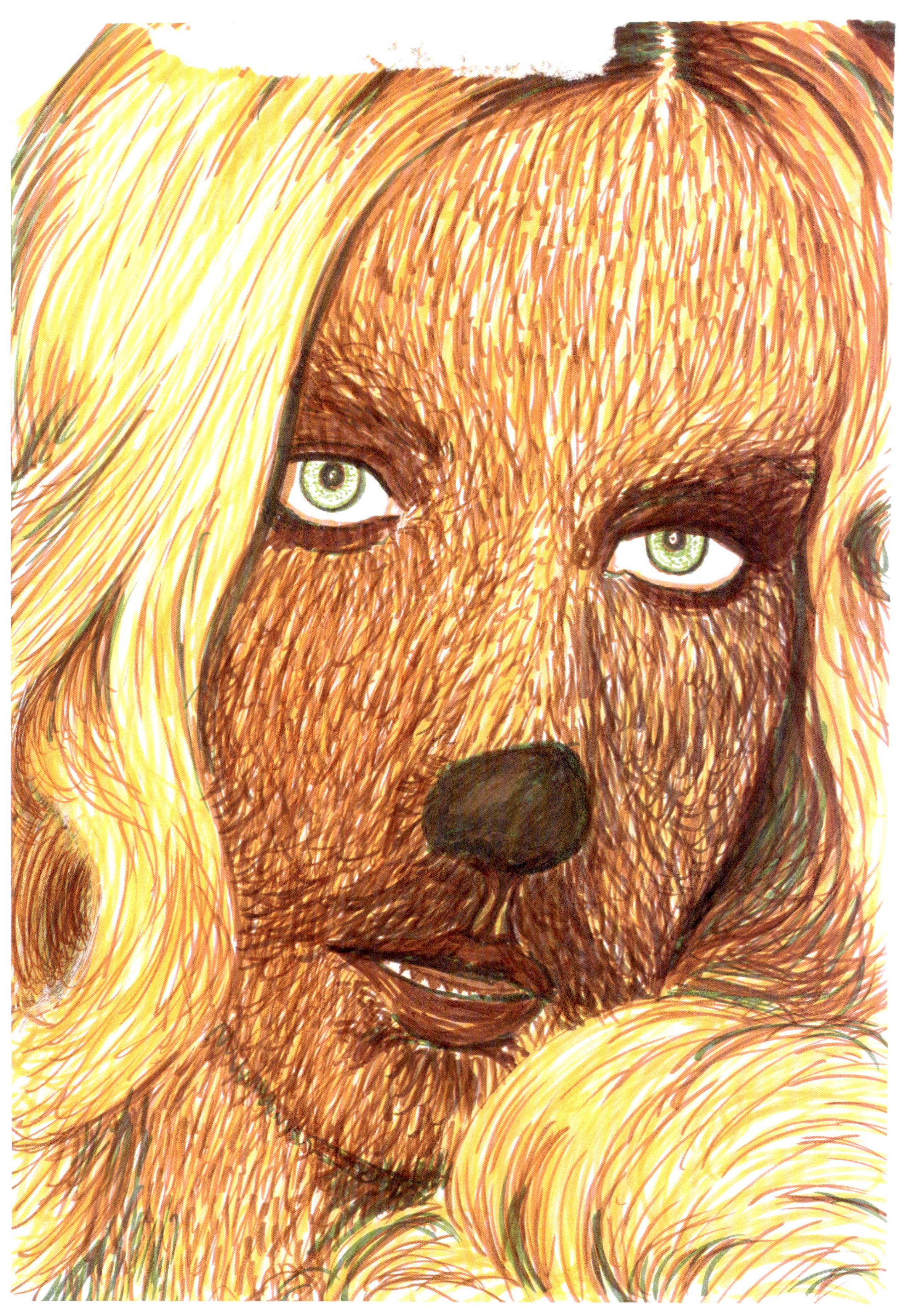

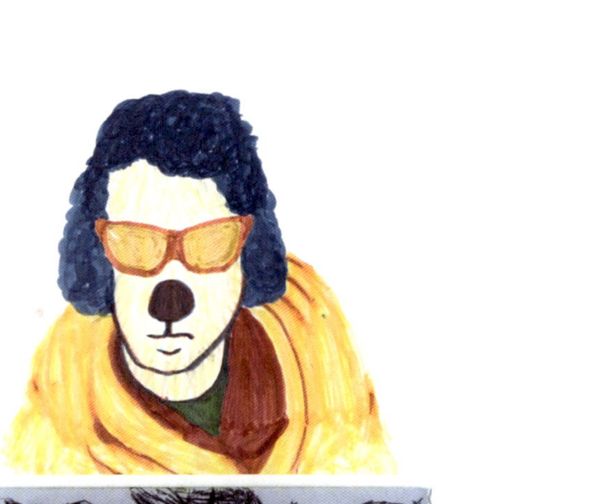
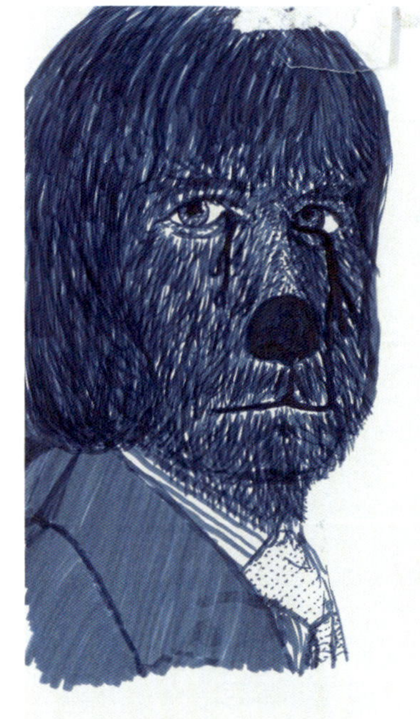

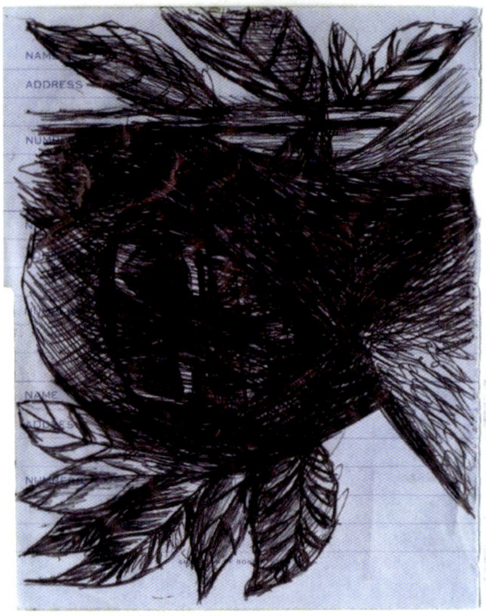

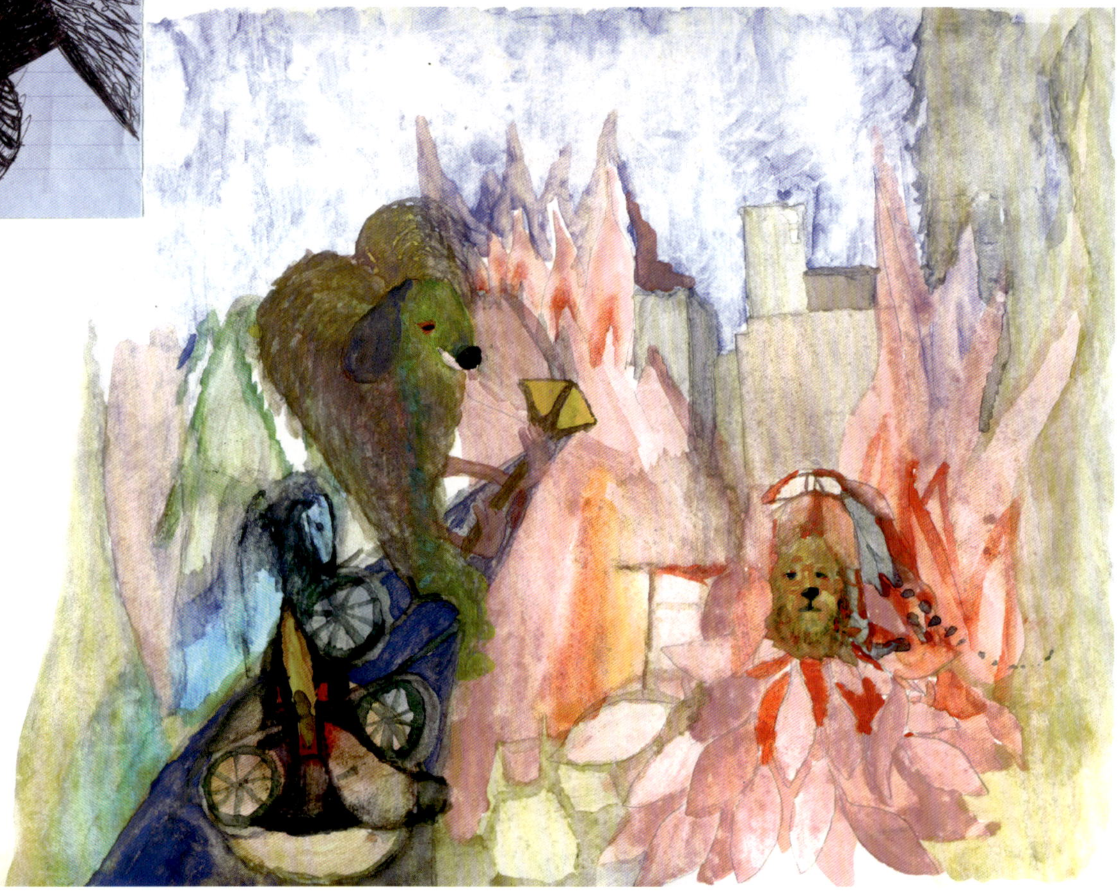

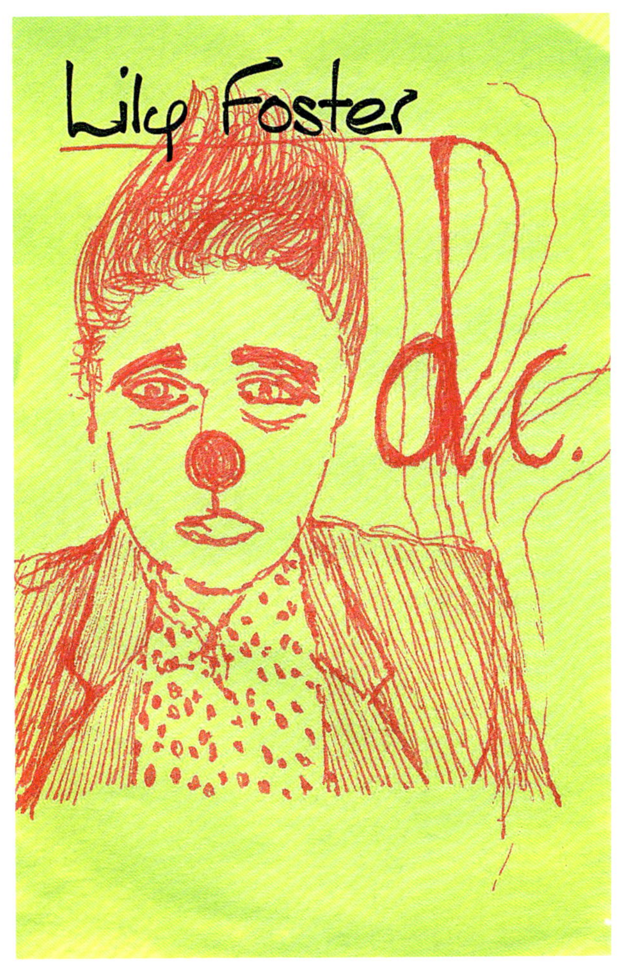

Lily Foster
d.c.

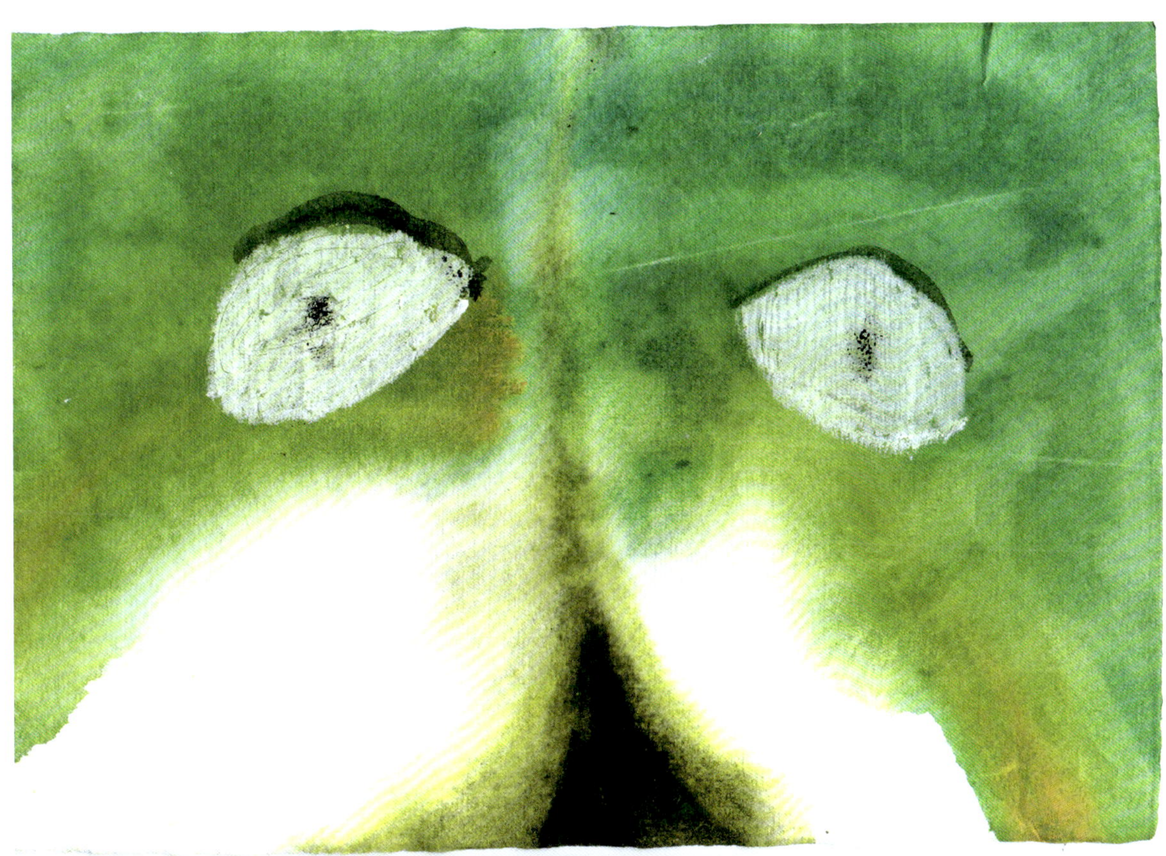

1. Intro

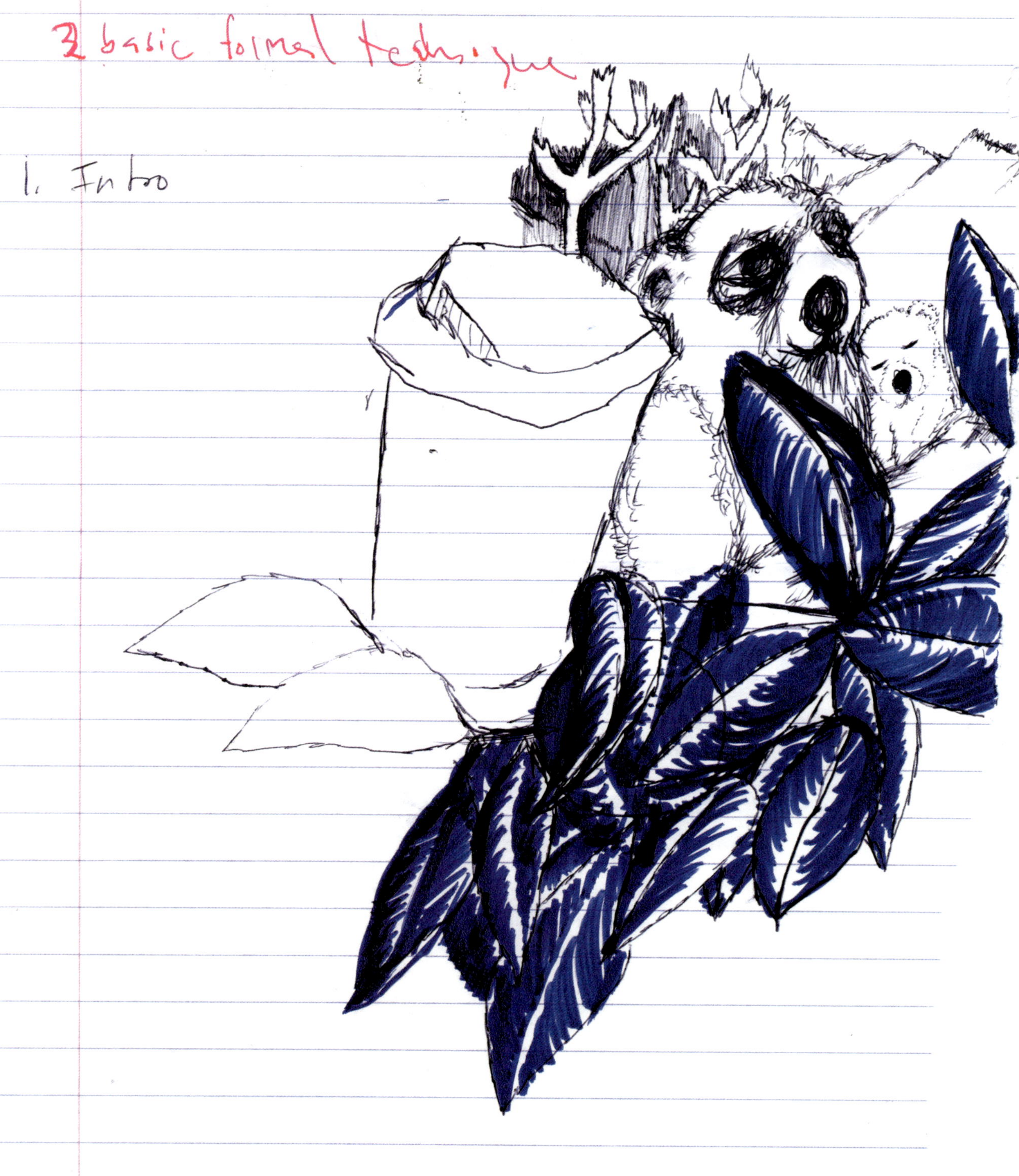

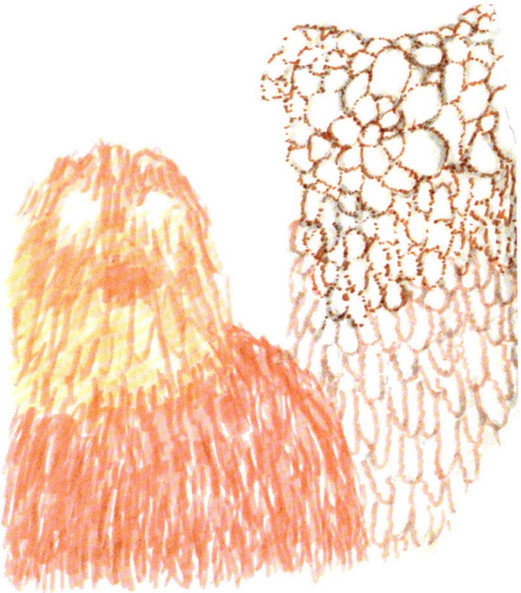

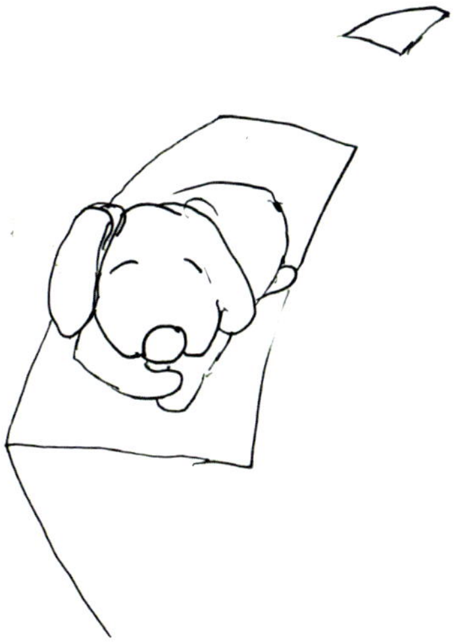

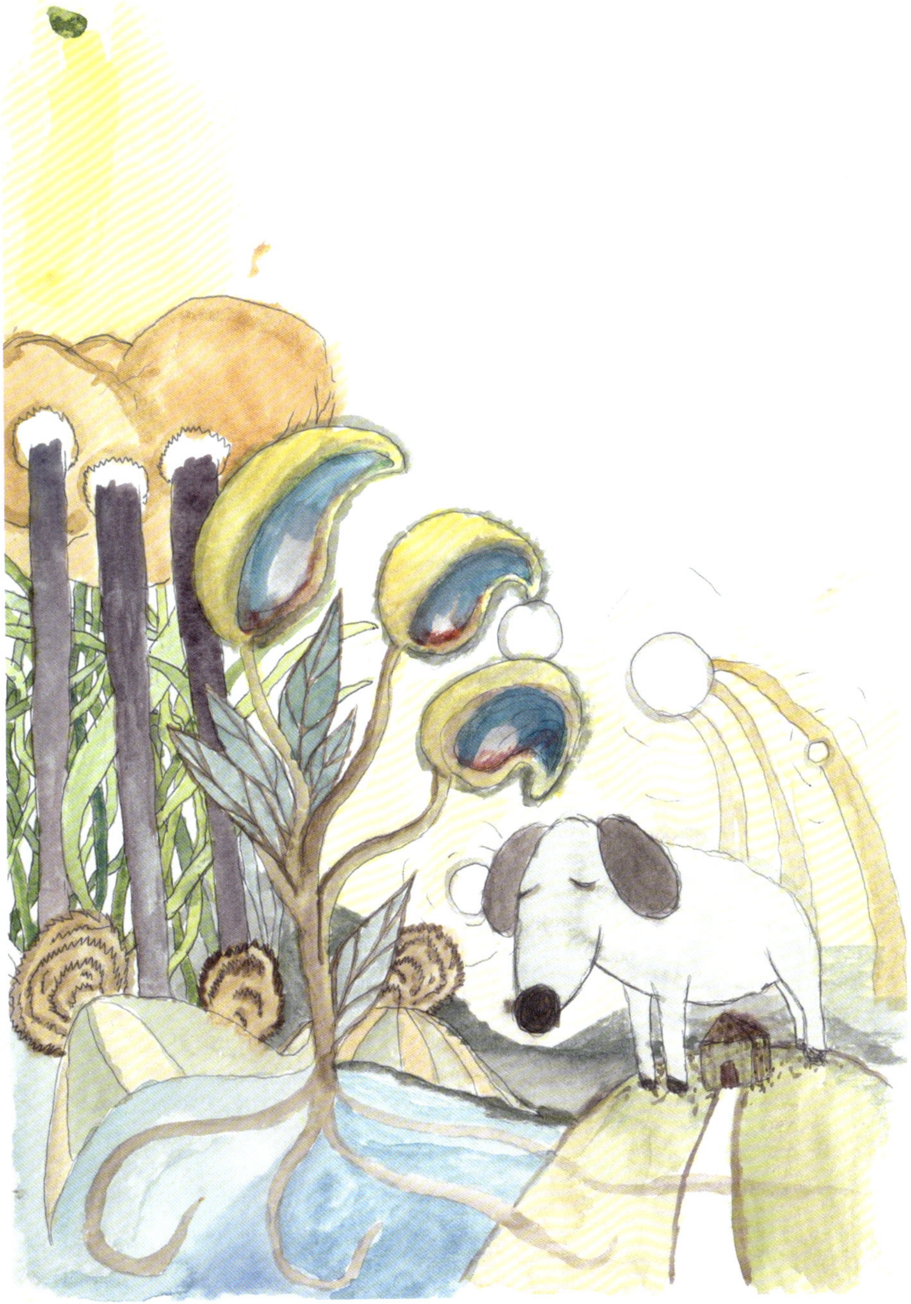

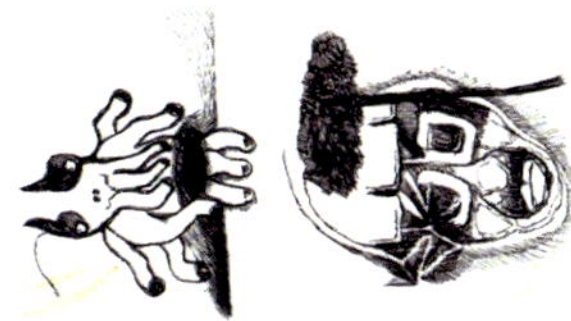

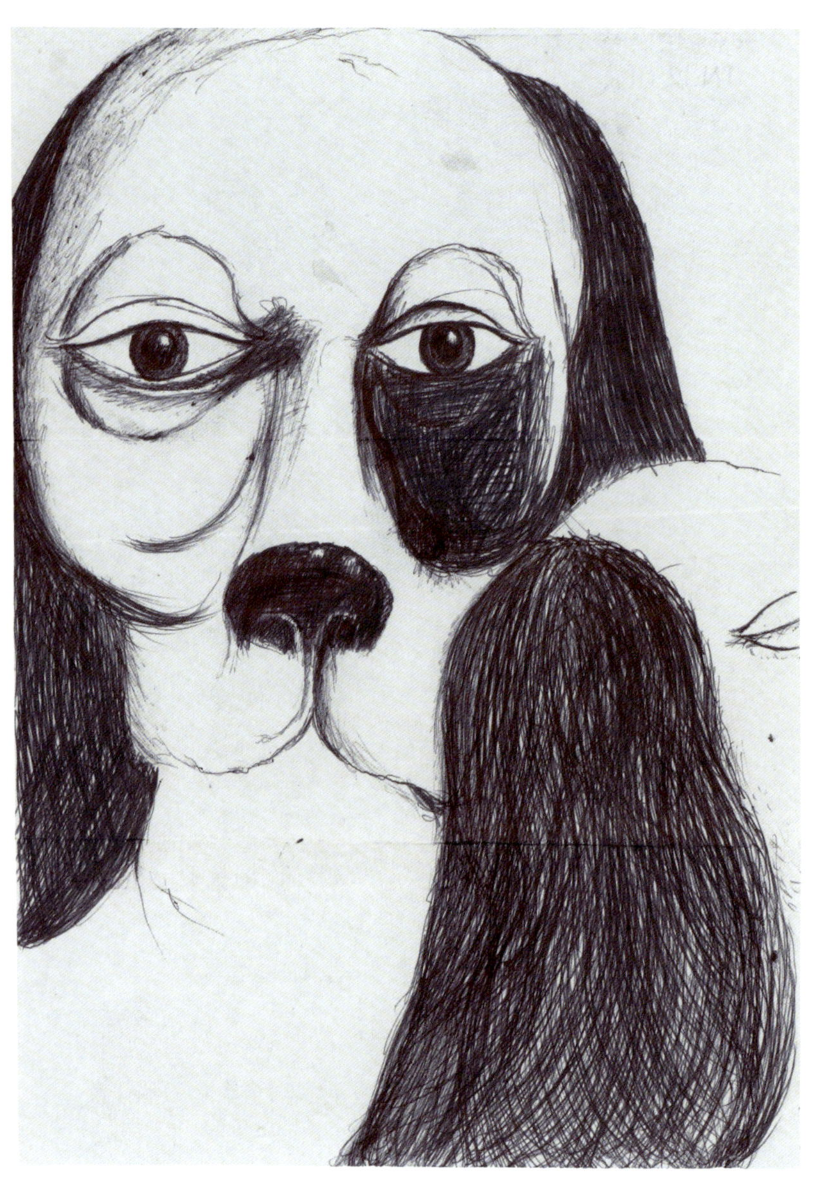

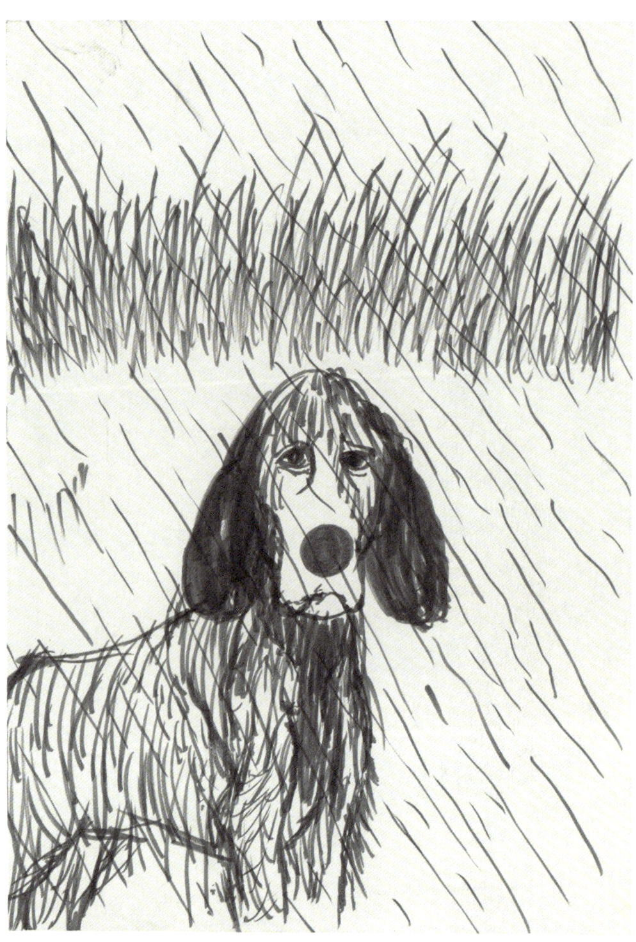

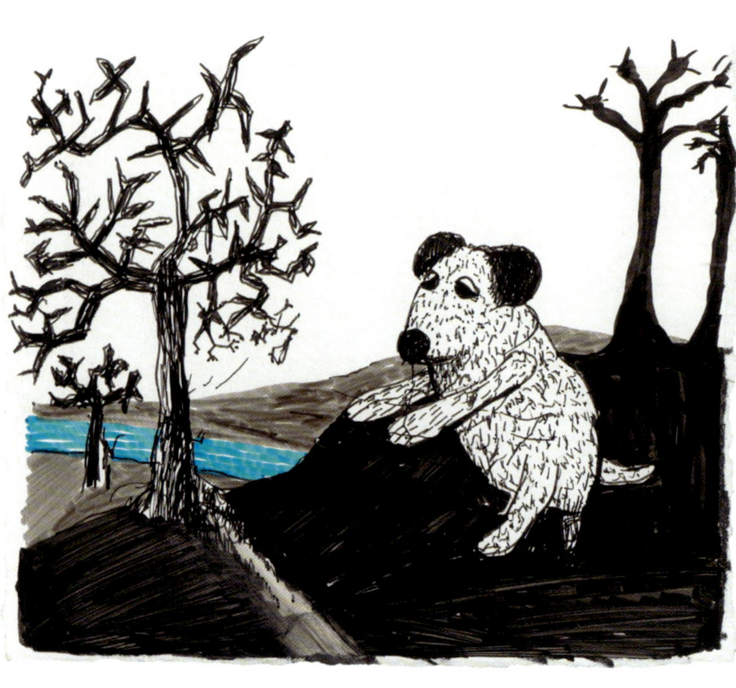

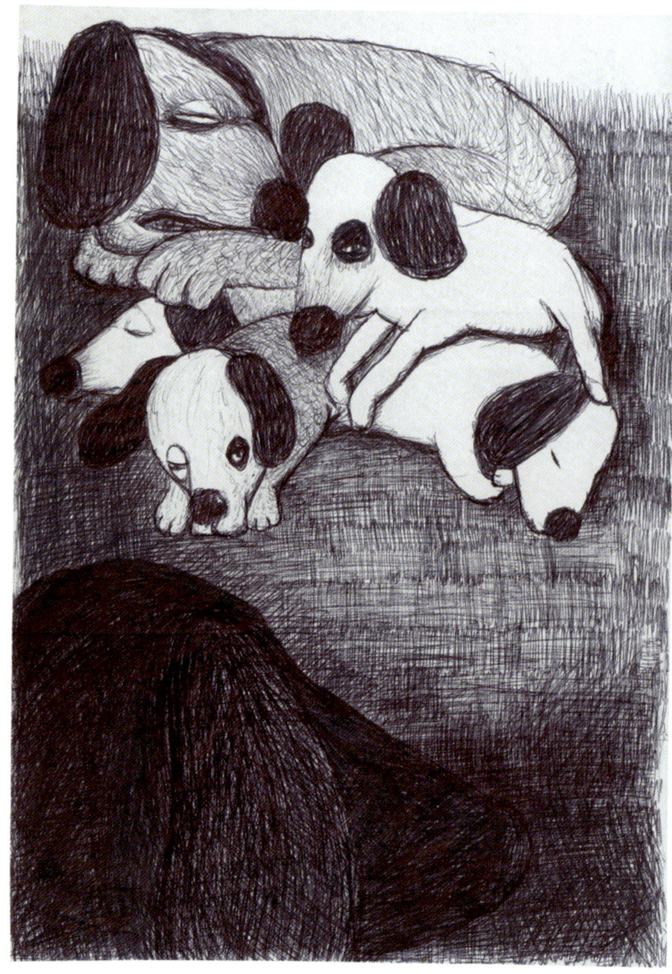

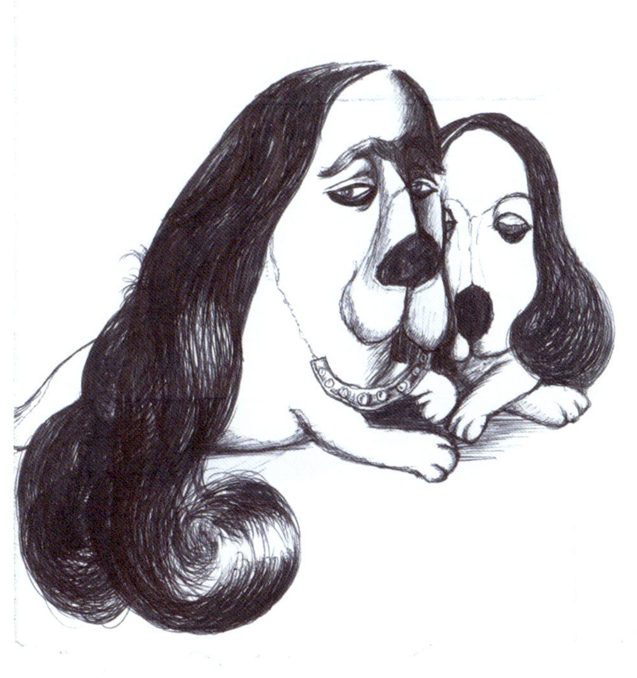

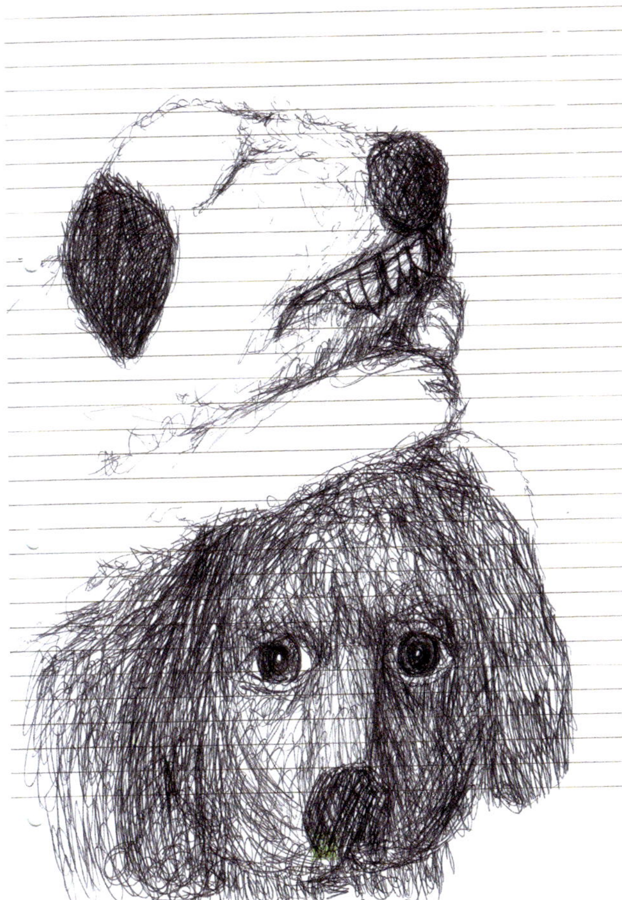

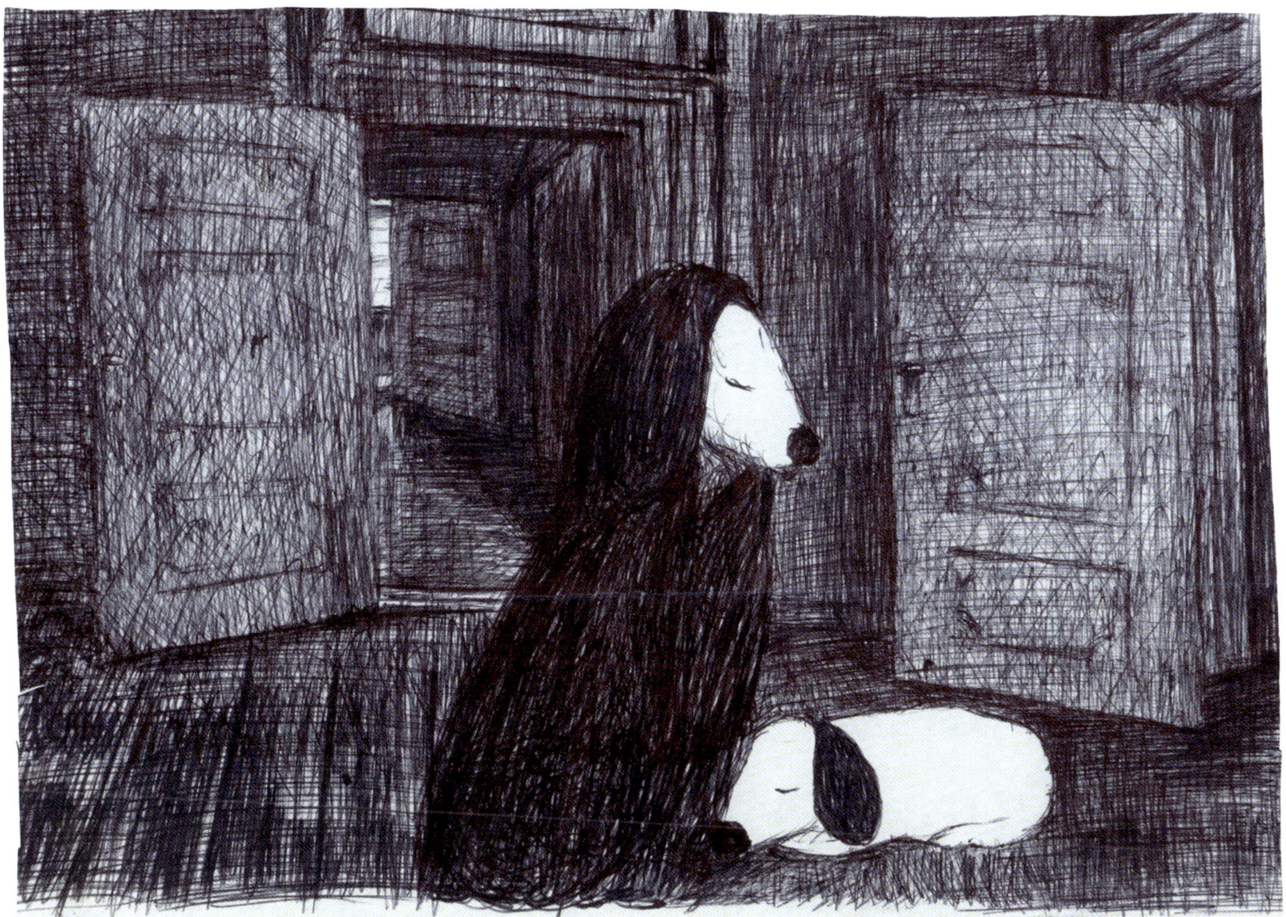

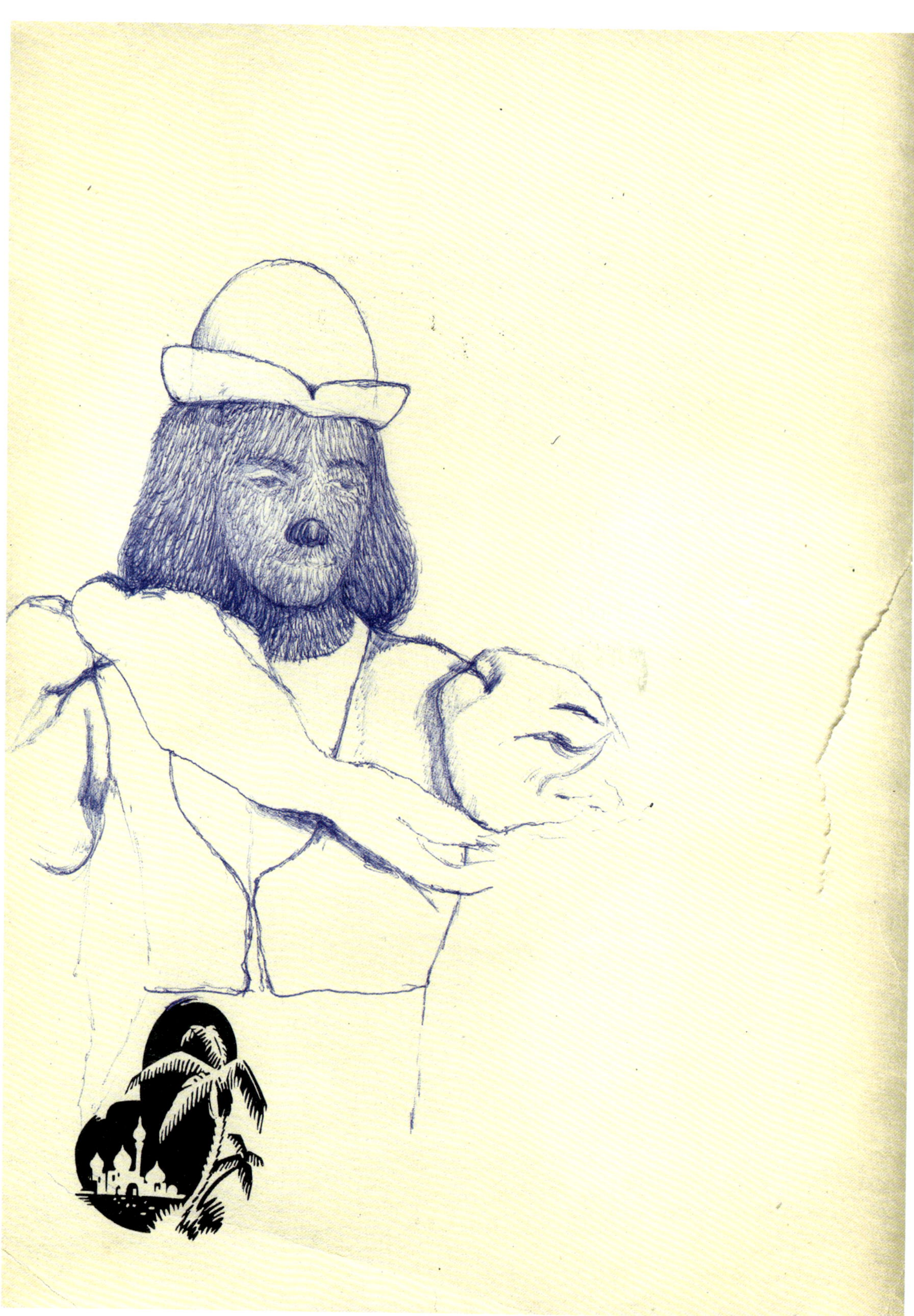

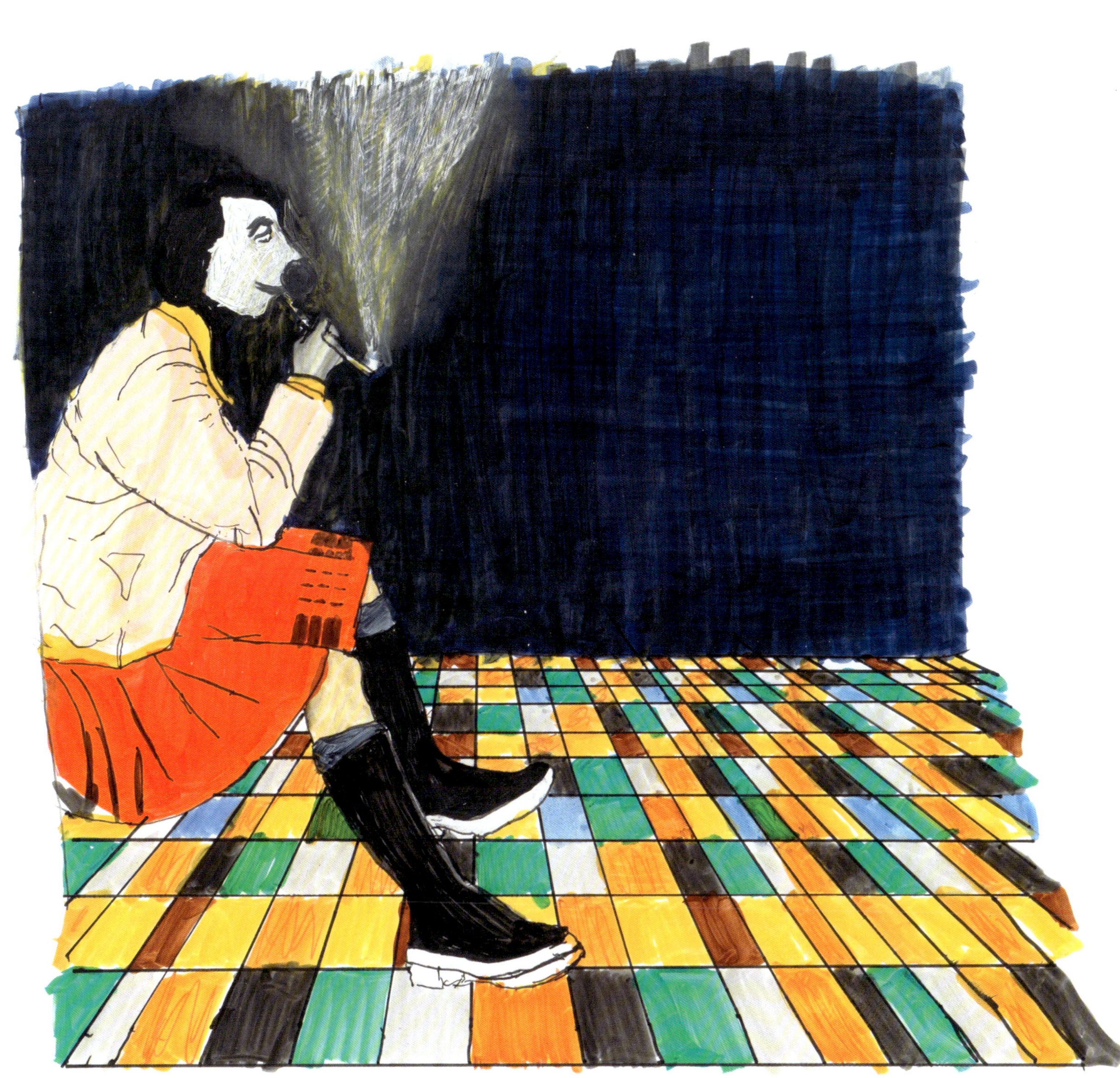

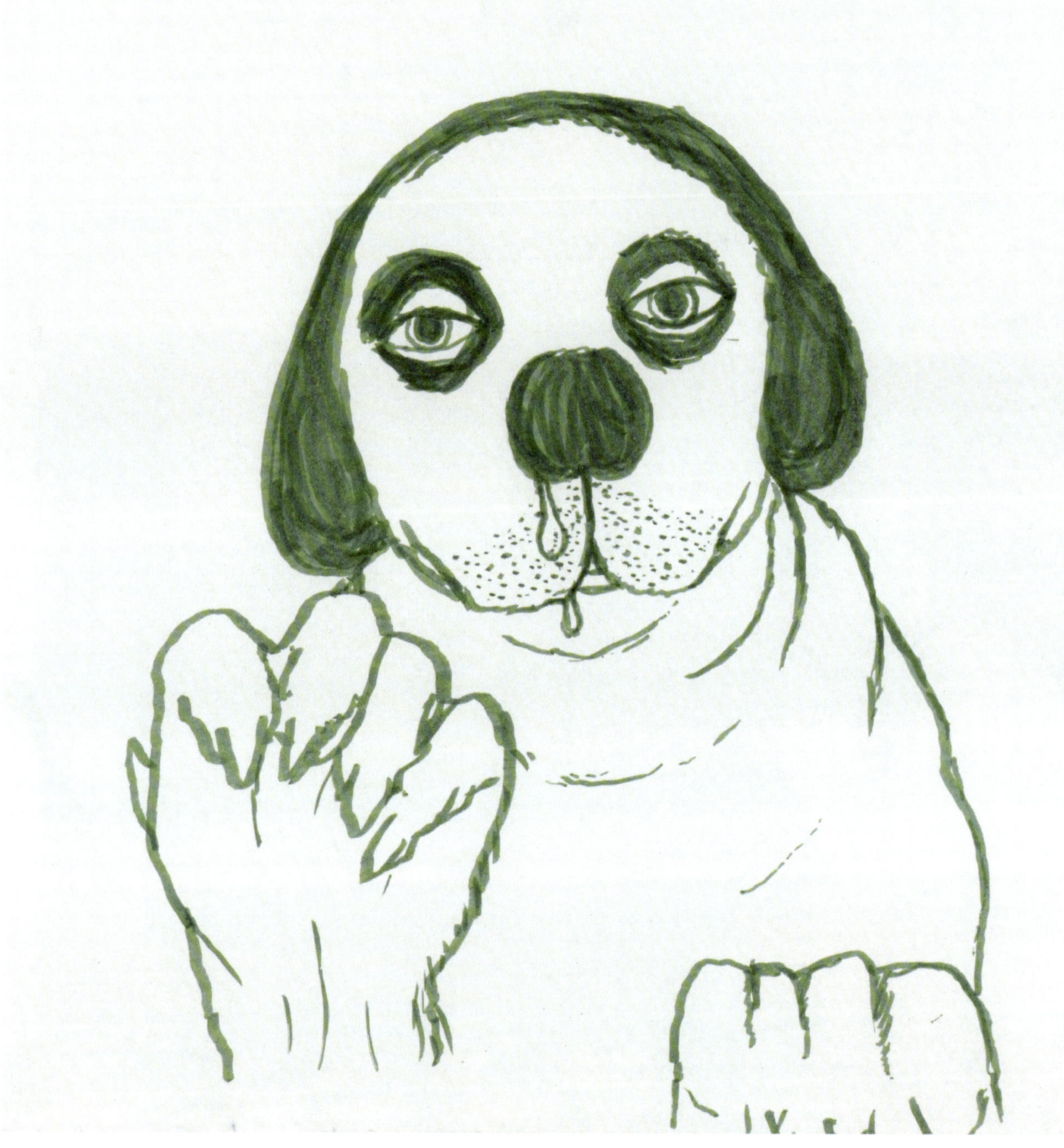

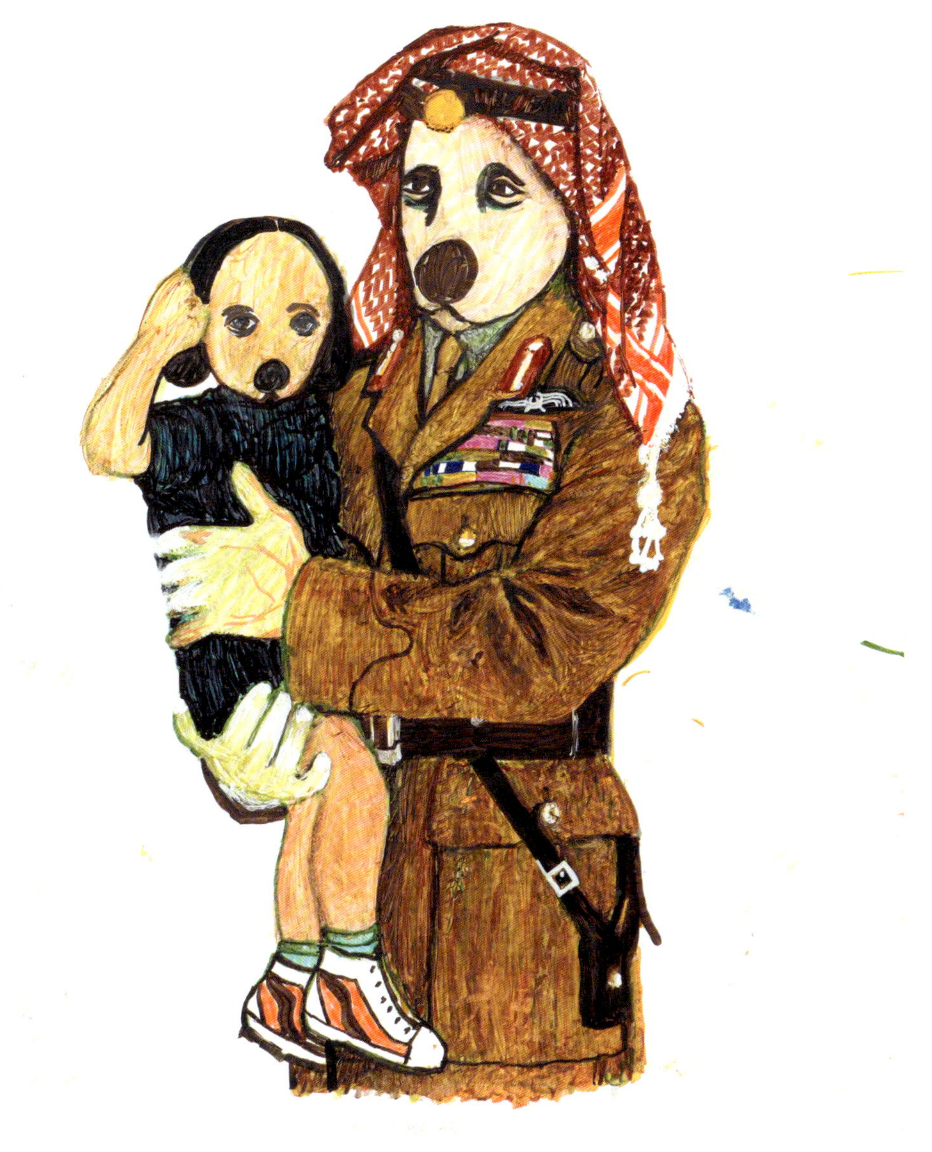

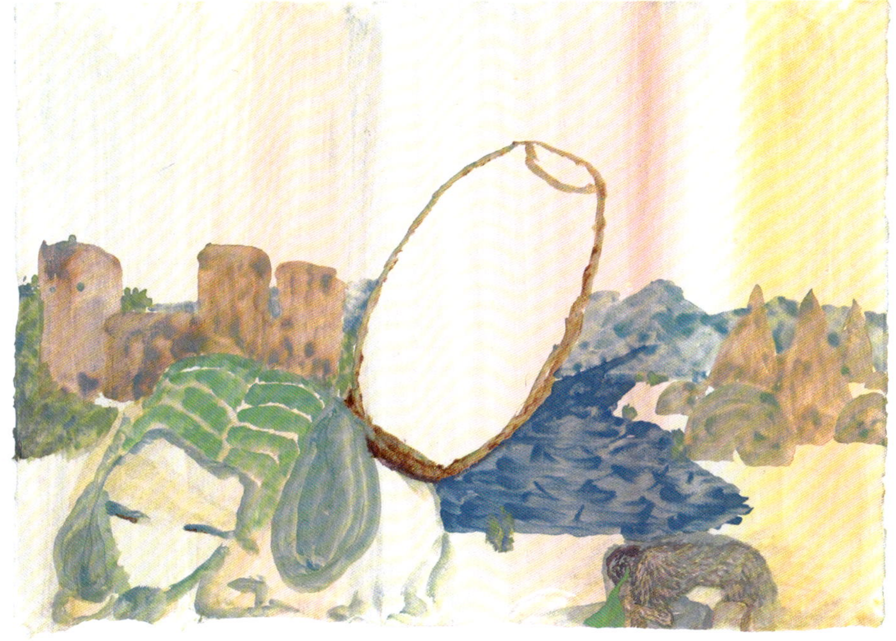

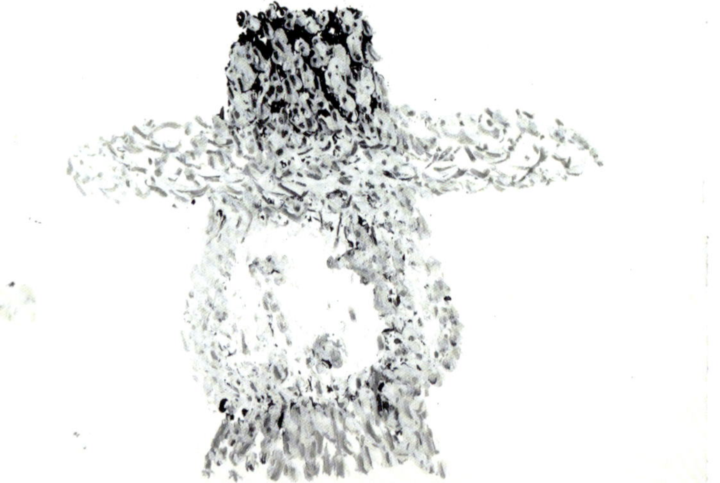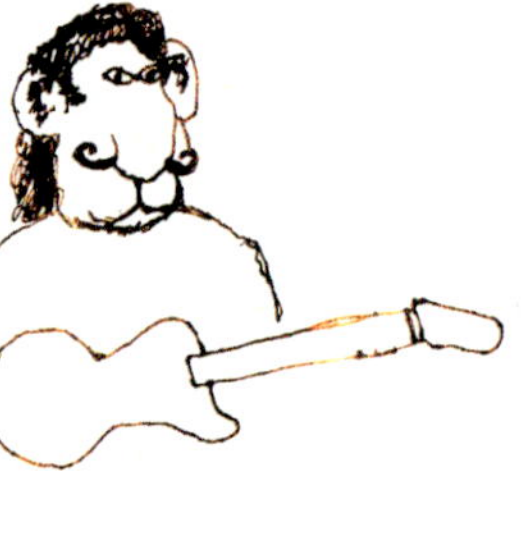

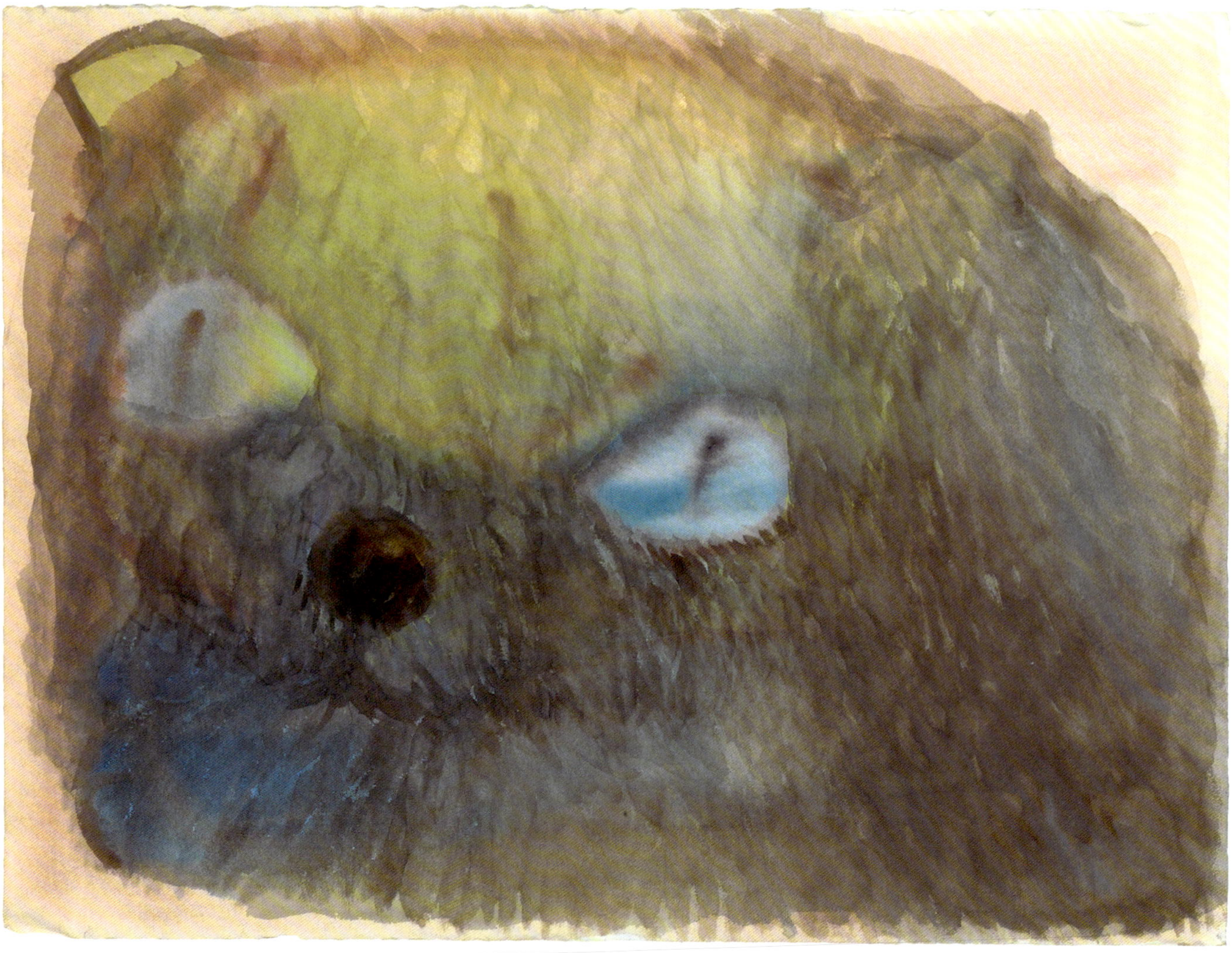